Guide to Travel and Recreation

The Danbury Press

WOMAN ALIVE

Guide to Travel and Recreation

by Maureen Matheson

Inter ibérica, S.A. de Ediciones

Series Coordinator: John Mason
Design Director: Guenther Radtke
Picture Editor: Peter Cook
Editor: Susan Allen
Copy Editor: Mitzi Bales
Research: Elizabeth Lake
         Sarah Waters
Consultants: Robin Dewhurst
            Beppie Harrison
            Jo Sandilands

Contents

Planning a family vacation? Then this helpful travel guide is a must. Filled with tips and hints on travel, it is also an aid for general recreation and shorter trips. Unlike those glowing travel brochures that give only the advantages of vacations described, this guide is comprehensive and unbiased. You'll find the pros and cons of all kinds of vacations, plus information on how and when to go; what's best for children of various ages; how to keep expenses down; and what to do on weekends or rainy days when the children are restless. Anyone can do exciting things when money is no object, but it takes ingenuity and imagination to get the most out of a vacation on a budget. This book was written with just that fact in mind.

Away From it All!

Almost from the time men began living in cities they have been finding ways to get away from them for a refreshing change.

Below: this ancient mosaic shows Romans relaxing in a country village outside Rome.

Above: medieval French noblemen and their ladies enjoying a day in the country.

Below: the practice of "taking the waters," as shown here in a 19th-century painting of Bath, England, was a form of health cure.

Above: bathing in the sea too was at first advocated mainly as a health treatment.

Below: it didn't take Victorian children long to discover the fun of beach play.

Right: today, getting away from it all for a break is possible—and vital—for us all.

Early Vacationers

Early holidays were purely a do-it-yourself business, requiring money, determination, and considerable imagination to achieve.

Right: a party of 19th-century amateur mountain climbers in the Savoie region.

Below: Victorians at the seaside, a detail from a painting by William Powell Frith.

Right: walking parties were a favorite way for many respectable 19th-century families to enjoy the pleasures of the countryside.

Below: from his first 1841 excursion in England for a temperance party, Thomas Cook went on to provide this tour to Paris.

Above: a contemporary photograph of a group of skiers in 1905 enjoying the pleasures and great beauty of the slopes in Switzerland.

The Sightseers

Before the camera brought the sights of Europe to every village around the world, the only way to admire the monuments of culture or the famous art treasures was to make the trip to see them for yourself.

Below: thousands of medieval pilgrims made long and arduous journeys to visit the relics and holy places of Christianity, often encountering hazards and hardships.

Right: Shelley, here visiting the Baths of Caracalla in Rome, was one of the many writers of his century who criss-crossed Europe in pursuit of inspiration.

Right: during the 18th century the Grand Tour became a rich man's status symbol, showing that he possessed considerable means and a fine sense of culture—as well as endurance to stand up to primitive travel.

Above: as the numbers of tourists increased, enterprising local citizens obliged by producing the thrills in the Catacombs of Paris that the foreigners apparently sought.

Below: with all the wonders of modern communications, legions of tourists can report that nothing compares with seeing the splendors of antiquity for themselves.

Getting There

For the tourist of yesterday, as of today, how to travel was an intriguing question, not to be decided without due consideration.

Right: jaunts on horseback were a familiar idea, if uncomfortable for long distances.

Below: for centuries, the dreadful possibility of bandits was a real threat to travelers almost everywhere in Europe. ©S.P.A.D.E.M.

Bottom: railways, like this early English one of 1833, opened up the world of travel.

Above left: the motor car produced even more revolutionary changes in transport.

Above right: early this century, splendid ocean liners provided a gracious crossing.

Below: today's travelers have the choice of land, sea, or air transport, readily and inexpensively available, to whisk them away in conditions that their predecessors would marvel at as unbelievably luxurious.

Vacations of the Future

In the search for new and exciting ways to spend a holiday, tourists are spreading out all over the face of the wide world.

Right: package tours to the Antarctic are already a possibility for the adventurous attracted by austere and frozen beauty.

Below: tours now reach the foot of the Himalayas—perhaps next, the summits.

Right: the vast world under the surface of the oceans has long attracted men, and the popularity of skin-diving may well lead to amateur exploration of the deeper levels.

Below left: the inaccessibility of the deep jungle (this one is in South America) serves as a challenge to pioneering types who relish the chance to test their endurance.

Below right: surely the last word in holidays of the future would be a tour literally out of this world. Some enterprising airlines have already issued tickets, like this one, reserving a seat on their first passenger service to the recently explored moon.

Know All Ye by These Presents that

A.L. READING

has become a certified member of Pan Am's

"FIRST MOON FLIGHTS" CLUB

66866 _James S. Montgomery_

Number   Vice President, Sales

What is a Vacation?

A generation ago, most Americans were lucky if they could take a week off for an annual family vacation. Today, with vacation time averaging two or three weeks a year, and three-day weekends occurring more often, family travel and recreation is possible all year round.

Do we really take advantage of our increased leisure time, however? Do we instead use it merely to catch up on unfinished work, unnecessary chores, or uninspired idleness? For a surprising number of people, the enjoyment of leisure time is much diminished by anxiety and boredom. Remember the last time you woke up on a crisp, fall morning longing to get out into the countryside, only to end up indoors cleaning the attic, or polishing the silver? How often have you thought: "Next year we'll do something different on our vacation," and then found yourself back at the same familiar lake or beach resort?

Nobody in today's hectic world should seriously question the wisdom of taking breaks—whether a full-blown European vacation, or a weekend excursion. What we should question is how we can make our vacations more memorable, and more fun for everyone. This is all the more true of family vacations, because from that first speculative moment when you start tossing ideas back and forth, you are setting in motion a genuine family adventure. You're not just escaping together from the kitchen sink, the schoolroom, factory floor, or office desk. You're planning a joint venture into a whole new world, where you will be thrust suddenly and constantly into one another's company. Family relationships are bound to be intensified by taking them out of the familiar home background, and replanting them in a strange environment. Inevitably there will be tensions and disagreements, but the satisfaction of shared experiences and discoveries can be immensely enriching. As countless families have found, it is this intangible element that heightens and emphasizes even somewhat ordinary incidents, and makes them the stuff memories are made of. Who isn't convinced that the sun never stopped shining through all those wonderful childhood summers?

Vacations are all things to all people. No two persons, even within the same family, share the same ideas about what to do and where to go. So, naturally enough, good family vacations don't just happen. They have to be planned with love, persuasion, tact, and skill. The range of possibilities these days is so wide, however, that you're certain to find one with something for everyone. We'll be giving you an idea of the number and types of vacations you have to choose from, as well as tips and hints that can only add to your enjoyment. But before we get to specific types of vacations, what about the basic factors that affect every family's travel and recreation plans? Chief among these, of course, is the question of planning itself. As far as possible, children should be considered on equal terms with the adults. Their wants and needs, their particular habits and interests must be taken into account. Most

The excitement of your vacation starts as you dream over the ways you may spend those free weeks: a lazy break from ordinary routine, an energetic burst of outdoor activity—or maybe just the time away from home in a new and different place.

parents would agree with this simple philosophy as an everyday matter, yet it's surprising how often these obvious factors are somehow neglected when vacation time rolls around. As parents who have ignored their children's wishes discover to their dismay, the success of any vacation depends on the enjoyment of *every single* member of the family.

With babies the family is at its most flexible. Confined to a portable bed, an infant is highly mobile and uncomplaining, and usually travels well by car, rail, or air. Since it can share a hotel room with parents, and needs only basic foods, costs are just marginally more than for two adults. Don't be put off by scare stories about traveling with babies. They are generally far tougher and more adaptable than we give them credit for.

The older children get, the more democratic vacation planning has to be. If you have teenage children, and the ordinary vacation just won't do any more, it may be time to ask yourself whether you're stuck in a rut. Have you outgrown your routine now that the children are older? Is it time for a radical change? Is this the moment to face facts, and let your eldest go their separate travel ways?

Most of today's teenagers are so independent that dictating vacation terms is simply declaring war. So here's a way of democratically planning your vacation, and having fun at the same time. Early in the year, get all the members of the family together, and sit down around the kitchen table for a special meal or favorite snack. Ask each person: "What would you like to

Today, more than ever before, the essence of a vacation for most of us is to leave the noise and pollution of city life behind us and, like the family shown here, relax amidst the quiet beauties of nature. This is the kind of vacation that soothes and refreshes body and soul.

A family vacation involves the whole family, and the happiest family vacations bring together the separate enthusiasms and interests of each family member, so that everybody feels they have helped to choose just where they go and what they do.

choices in planning a vacation, financial considerations often do not. Many people, however, mistakenly assume that any out-of-the-ordinary vacation costs far more than the usual two weeks at the seashore. This simply isn't true. There are hundreds of exciting, unusual vacations well within the means of most families on a budget, and many of them are described in later chapters.

Whether you are splurging this year, or have to trim your vacation budget to the bone, you will still probably be laying out a substantial sum of money. This means that you will have to budget for your vacation just like you budget for any major expenditure. The best policy, of course, is to have your funds in hand before leaving. Going now and paying later is not such an economy when you consider the interest charges, and many don't like to pay for a vacation when memories of it have already faded.

How you save for your vacation is between you and your will power. Probably the best method is to open a savings account exclusively for your vacation funds, and to make a deposit in it each week or month. That way you have the satisfaction of watching your travel funds grow while collecting the best interest rate on your savings. Another advantage of a separate savings account is that you can increase your deposits whenever your budget allows. Some people, however, prefer to save by means of "vacation club" accounts. You deposit the same amount of money in the account each week, and at the end of the year, the bank writes you a check for the amount you've saved. The major drawback is that few accounts of this type pay interest. In any case, pick the system that works for you, and stick to it.

do most?" Discourage gently, but firmly, those ideas that are clearly outside your family budget by suggesting more reasonable alternatives. For instance, an African wildlife safari may be wildly beyond your means, but a visit to one of the many safari parks around the country might be an acceptable substitute.

If the discussion breaks down into disorder and general disagreement this time, simply adjourn the meeting until another day. The aim is not to reach a final decision at once, but to give each person a chance to have his wants and needs considered, and to arrive, sooner or later, at a plan that satisfies the whole family. The participation of every member at the planning stage makes the best possible start to a vacation.

While interests generally leave you some

Budgeting is something every member of the family can help on. Since everyone likes to have some money to spend as he chooses, let everyone contribute to the family savings. Younger children can put by a bit each week from their pocket money, and older ones can take an odd job to earn a little spending cash. Some financial independence, however short-lived, adds another dimension to

Your bags are packed, the house is locked, your flight is called, and you're finally on your way— who hasn't had that bubbly feeling of expectancy as the long-planned-for vacation actually begins?

the experience of youngsters on vacation.

What happens when vacation time rolls around and there are simply no savings at all, or when you want to take a mini-trip during the year, and don't want to use money you're saving for the big trip? In cases like these, you might consider borrowing the cash for your vacation by taking out a personal bank loan, or charging your expenses on a credit card installment plan. While interest rates are generally high— about 18 per cent annually—many people find paying after the vacation easier than saving beforehand. As long as your family budget is healthy, borrowing can often be a sensible solution, especially if it means the difference between a family trip and no vacation at all.

You will probably have a good idea of just how much money you can afford to spend, but it's more difficult to judge exactly how far it will go. This depends on all kinds of things, such as the type and length of vacation, the country, transportation costs, and, of course, sudden whims and emergencies. It's always better to overestimate your total costs so you won't be caught short; but given average situations, and using a little care, it's surprising how far you can stretch your

travel cash. We'll be giving you a rough idea of the comparative costs of different types of vacations throughout the book.

How can you make the most of your family's leisure time together? There is no magic formula, but enjoyment depends not just on what you do and where you go—and certainly not on how much you spend—but also on a mixture of creativity, planning, spontaneity, and spirit. The spontaneity and spirit must, of course, be all yours. Tips on planning, and creative ideas for your family leisure time—whether a full-scale vacation, or a weekend break—are what this handy and useful book is all about.

Today the airplane has become the magic carpet for millions of vacation goers, carrying them off to places a hop, skip, and a jump from home, or half-way around the world to exotic foreign settings.

Traveling With Your Car

2

Flying may be quicker, sailing may be more sophisticated, and bicycling may be healthier, but for 90 per cent of all Americans, a vacation still means a trip in the family car. Why? It is simply the most economical, flexible, and convenient means of travel we have. There are no reservations to make or tickets to buy, no waiting for trains or buses, and, best of all, there are no schedules to meet. You are free to set your own pace.

America is crisscrossed by more than $3\frac{1}{2}$ million miles of roads—ranging from super

A car gives you freedom to explore otherwise hard-to-reach areas, and lets you start and stop as the fancy takes you.

Left: Great Salt Lake is one of the spots you would need a car to see.

Below: billboards often announce giveaway brochures, which are useful in planning your trip.

highways to winding country lancs—and driving them for pleasure has become a well-established national pastime. Chances are you're no stranger to some of the fun, and probably all of the frustrations, of car travel. If you have to travel with young children in the back seat, enjoying a car trip may seem an impossibility. Coping with car sickness, separating fighting youngsters, and answering for the thousandth time the nagging question, "Mommy, when do we get there?" can turn the most patient and loving parent into a raging tyrant. For those of us who have been caught in a 10-mile traffic jam, or stranded by engine trouble, driving for pleasure might seem, at best, a hollow laugh. But pleasure is exactly what a car trip should be, and the aim of this chapter is to help you make your car trip as enjoyable and memorable as the most exotic or expensive vacation.

As with any vacation, the key to the success of your trip by car lies in the amount of time and energy you put into the planning. Your first step is to decide how much you

Above: planning your route in advance will save
you time and gas—and spare your temper as well.
Right: this shows how good planning pays off.
If you've done your homework, you will be on the
fast superhighway instead of the battered old road.

want to drive. If you're like Brian and Pat,
you may decide the car is merely a means to
an end. Before departure Brian carefully plots
the most direct route to the sun. When the
great day arrives, he packs the family into
the car, climbs into the driver's seat, and sets
off at a steady pace. Making only the most
essential rest and service stops, he reaches
their destination late that same day. Only
then does the family begin to relax.

Richard and Margaret, on the other hand,
take the view that getting there is half the
fun. When their long awaited vacation
arrives, they agree on an area they want to
visit, and set off at a leisurely pace. Along the
way they may wander down country lanes,
and end up at a small town fair, or be
attracted to stop awhile by the charms of
some unspoiled fishing village. They enjoy

surprise discoveries, spur-of-the-moment
decisions, and chance meetings. The essence
of their vacation is the freedom to roam,
stop, and stay as the mood—and the
byways—dictate.

The difference between the couples is
largely explained by the ages of their children.
Brian and Pat's two youngsters are one and
five. While the baby, like most infants, is a
surprisingly good traveler, and content to
sleep most of the day in her car bed, her
five-year-old brother is a less happy passenger. He is too old to sleep most of the trip,
and too young to spend long hours cooped
up in the car without becoming bored and
restless. By contrast, Richard and Margaret's
two children are teenagers who enjoy
impromptu plans, exploratory detours, and
constant changes of scenery as much as their

parents do as a way of traveling by car.

If you're not sure how your children will react to a long car trip, try a weekend run first to see what problems arise. You might find, for example, that your youngster would be able to cope better if you break up the journey instead of driving steadily for nine or 10 hours straight. Remember, there is no right driving pace, but only the best one for your own family. There is, however, a wrong traveling pace. Day-and-night driving, trying to cover too many miles in a single day, and frantic speeding to make up for lost time will spoil everyone's vacation pleasure, and endanger the safety of your family. Most experts recommend 300 miles a day as a reasonable limit. So be realistic when planning the length of your trip, and your day-to-day mileage.

Once you have chosen a destination, write for information to the touring department of any major oil firm, or the Automobile Association of America (AAA) if you are a member. Tell them the areas you are interested in visiting, your point of departure and destination, and whether you prefer to travel by the most direct, or the scenic route. At no cost to you, they will send a map marked with the best route for your individual trip, as well as up-to-date information on road construction and detours that could save you precious vacation time. These complimentary services (the AAA charges a small fee for nonmembers) cover all areas of continental North America as far south as Panama. Check the telephone directory for the address of your local AAA office. Your neighborhood gas station can give you the address of its supplier's travel center, or will provide you with a preaddressed postcard.

Gather your whole family around the table, and trace your vacation route on the map. What states will you be passing through? What towns are you likely to stay in? What points of interest are within easy reach? You don't have to schedule every minute of your itinerary, but pinpointing the sites you want to visit, and mapping the best access routes can save you hours of aimless driving, inflated gas bills, and the disappointment of arriving at your destination five minutes before closing time.

Let's assume you are planning a trip from Atlanta to Montreal, and have decided to spend a week of your vacation visiting western Pennsylvania. A note to the Pennsylvania Tourist Bureau in Harrisburg will bring you an assortment of brochures on historic and tourist areas. From all the interesting spots, you might choose to spend a few days in the Pennsylvania Dutch Country, and also visit Gettysburg National Cemetery. Now write for more detailed information to the local tourist office—in this case the Pennsylvania Dutch Tourist Bureau. In most instances, the prompt response and variety of information provided will delight you. You'll find you can visit a rural farm museum near Lancaster, take a ride on the oldest short-line railroad in the country, or attend a music drama on the lawn of Ephrata Cloister—a remarkable retreat dating from 1732. From the bureau's calendar of events, you may find your visit coincides with a local auction, or annual fair. The accompanying restaurant and food guide will not only describe the traditional cooking of the Pennsylvania Dutch, but will also tell you where you can sample the best apple butter and shoofly pie.

State and regional tourist boards and local chambers of commerce are in the business of promoting their special points of interest, and are the best starting points for researching any trip. (See page 142 for addresses of state and regional tourist boards.) If they can't give you the information you want, they will

28

Our immense country is so varied and scenic that you have any number of choices of where to go for vacation. Whether it's to see the spectacular Grand Canyon, visit the bustling and colorful San Francisco, or soak up the sun on a beach, a car will enable you to get there faster and easier.

usually refer you to someone who can. If you are traveling outside the United States, the Canadian Government Travel Bureau (Ottawa, Ontario), or the Mexican Government Tourism Department (Av. Juarez No. 92. Mexico 1, D.F.) will provide you with plentiful and useful tourist information.

What about special interests? If you are an arts-and-crafts buff, or just interested in buying some genuine local handicrafts, the American Crafts Council's booklet, *Craft Shops/Galleries USA*, will give you information on hundreds of centers throughout the

29

country. Are you and your husband antique hunters? The American Antique Association, or a magazine like *Connoisseur*, can tell you of special auctions or shops in the area you are visiting. The same holds true for most special interest or professional associations, so don't hesitate to write. If you're not sure such an organization exists, or if you don't know where to write, visit your local library and check the Directory of American Associations.

An innovative guide for car travelers is the Auto Tape Tour, designed to appeal to both children and adults. Using colorful stories, music, and actual bird and animal sounds, the tapes will guide you through the highlights of various historic sites and national parks in the United States and Canada. You can rent both tape and tape player for a nominal fee from Auto Tape Tours, 565 5th Ave., New York, N.Y. 10017.

Choosing the right accommodation for your family can add immeasurably to the success of your vacation. Finding a motel to stay in is rarely a problem—their approach is usually signalled by large billboards and blinking neon lights. But a night in a regular motel can put a big dent in your vacation cash. Why not try one of the new budget motels that are springing up around the country? By eliminating most of the frills associated with motels—swimming pool, color television, restaurants, and such—they give you a clean, if simple, room for half the cost of their more luxurious rivals. Among such budget motels are Econo-Travel Motor Inns (Virginia), Scottish Elms (Tennessee), Days Inns (Georgia), and Motel 6 (California).

Motels may be easy to spot, but many other types of accommodation are not. Where do you find those quaint country

Staying in luxury motels that offer you private swimming pools, game facilities, and other conveniences is undoubtedly pleasant. But, except for the new budget motel chains, the cost of such accommodation is a drain on the budget. There are not as many budget motels as others, so you must be sure to make reservations in advance.

inns and private guest houses you hear so much about? Once again, local tourist boards and local chambers of commerce are usually your best source of information. They can not only tell you about small, out-of-the-way tourist homes, but can also alert you to unusual accommodations, such as a stateroom on the Queen Mary (now a luxury hotel docked in San Diego), or a motel made up of converted railroad cars (near Lancaster, Pa.). If you'd like to stay with a local family, they can give you names and addresses to which you can write. A more expensive alternative, but usually well worth the extra cost, are the historic inns scattered throughout the United States. Many date from colonial or pioneer days, and are landmarks in their own right. For more detailed information on locations and rates, you can purchase a copy of *Historic Inns in the U.S.* from the Berkshire Society located in Stockbridge, Massachusetts.

Many people don't realize that several of our national parks provide accommodation for noncamping visitors. You can spend a night in a luxury inn in Yellowstone, in a picturesque lodge in Shenandoah, in a simple cabin in Mesa Verde, or in a hotel in Hawaii Volcanoes National Park. For information on facilities, costs, and reservations, write to the superintendent at the park you want to visit. A word about reservations. If you are traveling at the height of the tourist season, or if you have your heart set on staying at a particular inn or resort, reserve well in advance. If you haven't reserved, call ahead in the morning to the place you would like to stay that night, whenever possible. If you're trusting to potluck, start looking early in the afternoon. Nothing is more infuriating than having to pay an exorbitant fee for a nondescript

room because it's too late to keep looking.

In the excitement of mapping your route, planning sidetrips, and reserving accommodations, don't forget the most important factor in any motoring vacation—the car itself. Have your car serviced and thoroughly checked a week or two before you plan to leave. Explain to your garage attendant how far you will be going, and what road conditions you expect. If your route will take you over hot, desert highways, or into rugged, mountainous roads, he may suggest special precautions or minor adjustments that can prevent major problems later on. Be sure that seat belts, door locks, and windows function properly, that your jack is free from rust and your spare tire in good condition, and that all other necessary tools and spare parts are packed for emergencies. If you are driving a foreign or custom-made car, check with your car dealer about renting a manufacturer's spare parts kit. It could save you days of waiting for parts to be shipped to some small, out-of-the way town. Don't forget to check that your car insurance is adequate, and paid up.

What happens if you have a major breakdown despite precautions? Probably your first line of defense is the AAA. If you are not already a member, you should think about joining before your trip. In addition to its travel information service, the AAA provides members with a 24-hour road emergency service throughout the United States and Canada. This means that whether you break down on a crowded thruway in rush hour, or on a back country road in the dead of night, a repair truck will come in a hurry.

Gas credit cards, issued by most national oil companies, are another source of comfort when you're far from home. They are invaluable for unexpected emergencies and major repairs, and come in handy late at night when many gas stations refuse to make change, or even to accept cash.

If your car is to serve as a home away from home during your vacation, you should make it as comfortable as possible for the

Getting the car ready for a trip means more than just fitting everything in. It means making sure that the car itself is in top condition, and that vital items are packed where you can get at them.

Give the children as much room as possible in the back by keeping the floor clear of any luggage. Put down a thin layer of foam to make sitting or crawling more comfortable, and throw in a couple of old blankets and pillows for naps. Let them also have some favorite toys for quiet games.

Be sure you've included a spare tire and a jack, spare headlights, and a kit of emergency tools in case of breakdown.

Make sure that all your tires are in really good condition, and that you are carrying a good spare—if you need to use it you'll be glad that you checked it out.

First Check Your Car

Keep your luggage in the roof-rack securely covered to protect yourself against the weather or a passing thief.

Have your car thoroughly serviced a week or so before you leave to make sure everything is in proper working order.

However nice looking they are, slippery non-porous seat covers can be very uncomfortable if you're driving in hot, sunny weather. Try using removable fabric covers or ventilated cushions to avoid that unpleasant sticky feeling.

Keep tissues, a damp face cloth, fruit, and candy where they can be reached easily.

Bring along your car's instruction manual to consult in case of trouble. If only a small repair is needed, you might be able to save an expensive call for garage repair service.

whole family. Reserve the passenger space of the car for passengers. All luggage, loose packages, and sports equipment not needed on the journey should be packed in the trunk. To avoid last-minute confusion, test your trunk space a few days prior to departure. If your vacation gear simply won't fit, check with an auto supply store about renting a rooftop luggage rack. The more room you have in the body of the car, the more comfort for everyone, and the less danger of small children being hurt by shifting objects.

What can you do to make the car more comfortable for small children? The back of station wagons can be converted easily into a playing or sleeping area by spreading a thin layer of foam or a heavy quilt on the floor. You can create the same area in a sedan by placing sturdy boxes or miscellaneous luggage on the car floor up to the height of the rear seat, and then covering the surface with a soft quilt.

Once you have ensured your children's physical comfort, you are still left with the problem of how to keep them entertained on a long car trip. Take along a good selection of playthings—games, favorite toys, coloring books and crayons, cards, and picture and story books. Have a surprise grab bag of new games and small novelties to divert young children when they become particularly bored or restless. Be ready to start travel games, songs, and other entertainment you learned on car trips with your own

Traveling With Your Dog

Here are a few reminders for traveling with a dog. Attach an ID tag that not only has your name, address, and phone number, but also the phone number of a friend who can be reached at home while you are still on the road.

To cross into Canada, Mexico, and some states, you must have two certificates from a vet: one stating that your dog has had a rabies shot in the past six months, and one saying that the animal is in good general health.

Never leave your dog in the car with the windows shut—and in hot weather, park the car in the shade.

If your dog is too large to take on a plane in a carrying case, it must go with the baggage. Make certain, then, that it will be in a pressurized and heated compartment.

34

parents. Don't neglect to pack a generous supply of snacks—fruit, cookies and crackers, candy and gum, fruit drinks or soft drinks—to satisfy the huge appetites most children bring along on long journeys.

Give each child a special chore or responsibility. Put the youngest in charge of dispensing snacks, or tidying up the back seat. An older youngster can be responsible for keeping the maps, watching for road signs, or reading up on places of interest along the way. If your teenager is a licensed driver, give him a turn behind the wheel.

The inside of a car gets messy in no time, so carry a supply of plastic litter bags with you, and make sure they're used. Keep on hand the things you'll need all the time: baby paraphernalia, games and toys, snacks and cold drinks, tissues, premoistened towelettes, a well-stocked first-aid kit, and special insulated bags in case anyone gets travel sick. If you know your children are prone to car sickness, ask your doctor to prescribe a drug for it, or buy a nonprescription medicine recommended by your local druggist.

Auto theft and burglary are on the increase, and cars of vacationers are a prime target. When you leave the car by day, put everything of value into the trunk, close the windows, and lock all the doors. Never

Another big convenience of going by car is that it can help you to save on food costs. Pack a picnic lunch, pull into a designated rest stop, and have a stretch of the legs as well as your satisfying snack.

leave anything temptingly in view to attract a thief. When parking your car for the night, choose a well-lit street, or a secure parking lot.

When you're on the move, watch out for tiredness. It can creep up on you quickly. The best idea is to stop every two hours or so to stretch your legs, and have refreshments. Picnic lunches are more relaxing than restaurant meals for young children, and have the distinct advantage of being both economical and time-saving. Most long highways have grassy picnic areas equipped with tables and toilet facilities. If you are driving on a scenic road you can usually choose your own picnic spot, so whenever the weather permits, fix a light lunch in the morning, or stop at a delicatessen for sandwiches before you begin your day's trip.

Economy, adventure, new places and sights—these are the things a good car trip is made of. But for most of us, the joy of traveling in the family car can be summed up in a single word—freedom. Freedom to come and go as you please, to make unexpected detours, and to get to know America's countryside, people, and special charms at close hand.

Camping Vacations
3

Ask any child what kind of vacation he'd like best, and the chances are he'll reply without a moment's hesitation: "Camping!" For him it is the world of make-believe come true. Pitching a tent and cooking out of doors, sitting around a campfire under the stars, and creeping from his sleeping bag at the first hint of dawn—it's like being Daniel Boone, Geronimo, and Lewis and Clark all rolled into one.

But children aren't the only ones who love to camp. Over the past 20 years camping has become the favorite pastime of millions of Americans. If you long for fresh air and freedom, and a chance to unwind in a peaceful, natural setting, then camping is for you. Best of all, a camping trip will keep vacation costs to an absolute minimum.

This, however, is the idyllic side of camping. There is another picture, complete with collapsing tents, burned food, sleepless nights, faulty equipment, and crowded, noisy grounds—not to mention nature's total indifference to your vacation plans. Many a first-time camper has had his enthusiasm dampened by cold, rainy weather, swarms of pesty mosquitoes, and prowling animals. While little can be done about the perversity of nature, proper planning and the right equipment can alleviate most camping discomforts.

Unless you're an experienced backwoodsman, your most important piece of equipment will be some kind of shelter—either a tent, or one of the growing number of recreational vehicles. Tents come in more shapes, sizes, materials, and colors than ever before. Some attach to the back of your car or station wagon; some perch on top of a car,

For thousands of people, a vacation spent camping is a once-a-year chance to enjoy the pattern of clouds floating across a country sky, to smell the goodness of food cooking outdoors, and to sleep with the wind rustling the trees near your tent—and to relish the independence of a more self-sufficient life.

36

keeping you high and dry in wet weather; and some are freestanding, complete with separate living areas, one or more bedrooms, kitchen, and porch. Most tents have sewn-in floors, entrance flaps, heavy-duty zippers, and screened windows to keep you safe from the elements as well as crawling and flying pests.

Just how dry you remain in rainy weather will depend on the material your tent is made of, and on how it has been treated to resist water and mildew. Cotton fabrics are very durable and water resistant, and the "dry finishing" process, while expensive, is the best weather treatment. Make sure the tent you choose is easy to set up, and roomy enough for your family to sleep and move around in comfortably. Clear floor space and separate rooms make it much easier to cope with young children in wet weather, and to find storage space for all the gear you can't leave outside, or in the car. After buying your tent, take it home and practice setting it up in the backyard. Practicing ahead is a good idea with any new or unfamiliar equipment, in fact. You may feel like an idiot, but discovering defects, and ironing out any problems at home, can save unpleasant surprises once you reach your campsite.

The newest thing on the camping scene is the recreational vehicle—the rec vee or RV as it is usually called. If your budget can stand it, an RV might be the perfect answer to your camping needs. The simplest and most economical model is the camping or tent trailer, a boxlike structure towed on wheels behind your car. At a turn of a crank, the box opens to become a full size tent already conveniently off the ground. Many camping trailers have winged platforms to accommodate double beds. The more luxurious models have built-in tables, cushioned seats, and kitchen equipment. The tent trailer and its big brother, the familiar travel trailer, have one big advantage over other RV's. Once you've found a site, you can unhook the trailer, and go exploring where you wish in your car. Their disadvantage is that they are almost always

difficult to maneuver on rugged and winding roads. With larger trailers, which can range from the traditional, rectangular shaped vehicle to sleek, aircraft-style models, you have the added problem and expense of matching trailer and hitching equipment to the size and weight of your car.

The second type of RV avoids the towing problem by having the living quarters built right onto the body or chassis of a truck. This type is much easier to maneuver than trailers, and can be taken on any road you'd drive in a car. A popular model with young families is the converted van, probably because it makes an ideal second car for hauling children, or weekend shopping. It can be equipped as simply or as elaborately as your budget will allow, either by a firm that specializes in this kind of work, or with a do-it-yourself conversion kit. Some truck campers are merely shells built onto the back of a pickup, but in the more elaborate models you can expect to find full

Above: the familiar house trailer gives you most of the comforts of home, plus mobility— and you can take the car alone if the trailer is too awkward at times.

Left: a trailer vacation especially suits a family with young children—and the pet dog can go, too.

Far left: it must be a great way to go if one can judge by the many places this much-traveled camper truck has been.

kitchens, built-in beds, and rooftop sun decks.

The largest and most luxurious recreational vehicle is the motorhome. It is as easy to drive as a truck camper, and as self-contained as a trailer. It usually comes equipped with every imaginable comfort— from a full bath and streamlined kitchen, to custom-designed living and sleeping areas. The cost of one of these rolling homes on wheels? About $100,000! But for many people the built-in comforts of an RV are the antithesis of real camping. For them, camping means tents, sleeping bags, outdoor cooking, and, most of all, getting away from a chrome-and-steel environment. You can have this back-to-nature urge without doing away entirely with creature comforts. This is where the whole galaxy of modern camping gear has made such an impact. Camping in a tent no longer has to mean roughing it in any particular.

One of the first things you'll notice on a camping trip is how much better you sleep after a day of outdoor exercise—at least you will if your sleeping equipment is as comfortable as modern know-how can make it. Down or synthetic fiber-filled sleeping bags come in a variety of sizes to suit every member of your family. They are light in weight, comfortably warm, and fully water-repellant. (A sleeping bag should *never* be waterproofed, or it will trap moisture in your body and you will be soaked by morning.) What goes under you is almost as important as what goes on top. For additional insulation against cold and damp, you

dining and lounging, so giving double use.

Fresh air and exercise will not only make your family sleep better, but is also guaranteed to give them ravenous appetites. Satisfying that hunger can be a formidable task if you don't travel well equipped. Folding tables, coolers and refrigerators, and compact cooking utensils all play their part in making food preservation and preparation easy on a camping trip. Without doubt, however, the most indispensable item in your cooking gear will be a modern camp stove. Campfires are great to sit around, but for heavy family cooking, they are impractical. Many national and state parks ban fires during hot, dry seasons because of the danger to forests and foliage. Even when fires are allowed, you will discover that

Left: a shady patio is yours in a trice with the attachment of a portable awning and platform.

Right: the camper truck is one of the newest vehicles for giving you a home while you travel. It's easier to maneuver than a trailer because the living area is built onto a truck body. This also avoids the towing problems of the trailer.

can get modern, compact air mattresses, which sometimes come equipped with an electric pump for inflating them in a hurry. They can also deflate in a hurry if accidentally punctured, so lightweight foam pads are usually a better choice. They are bulkier than a mattress, but provide better insulation against cold and damp. If you prefer to be completely off the ground, shop around for a camp bed with a light, tubular frame and woven cover. Some beds can be adjusted to form upright or reclining chairs for

firewood is becoming increasingly hard to find. You can now get family-size stoves with several burners, adjustable flames, and oven attachments for more elaborate cooking. Most stoves are fueled by propane, or by white gasoline (mistakenly called "gas"). Though more expensive, propane is by far the safer, cleaner, and more compact of the two. It comes in disposable or refillable cylinders that you can buy in any camping, hardware, or department store.

Your camp fare can be as elaborate or as

simple as your time and tastes allow. Today, many campgrounds have food stores in which you can buy fresh meat and other perishables as you need them. Some even have restaurants, if you want a night out. But if you're camping in a wilderness area, you'll have to get by on what you bring with you. Unless you have a good camp cooler, you'd be wise to depend on canned, dehydrated, and freeze-dried foods, and not run the risk of eating tainted foods. This doesn't mean you must sacrifice either quality or variety in your camp meals. With the freeze-dried foods available in most camping stores you can enjoy complete gourmet meals—shrimp cocktail, beef stroganoff, and even ice cream.

The gasoline lantern is still the most popular form of camp lighting. Kerosene is the cheapest fuel, but you might find the smell objectionable. Most campers prefer using the same type of fuel for their lighting as they do for the stove, particularly if they can both be run on the same cylinder. You can do away with fuel problems altogether by using one of the new, battery-operated fluorescent lamps. Many models are rechargeable—you simply plug them into an electric outlet at home—and are not only attractive, but also a lot brighter than other forms of lighting.

If you are starting from scratch, equipping your family for a camping trip is an expensive and bewildering proposition. So don't rush off to the nearest camping store and depend on luck or intuition to help you make the right choices. Do some careful homework first: visit a camping show and compare different manufacturer's products, consult experienced campers about their favorite gear, subscribe to a camping magazine from which you can get information and critical comment on the latest equipment.

Another option open to both first-time and experienced campers is to sign up for one of the packaged camping trips offered by airlines and travel agents. For an all-inclusive price, they will fly you to the destination of your choice, provide all your camping equipment, plan your itinerary, and make campsite reservations. Of course, it's more expensive than a normal camping trip, but the cost is far below a comparable tour with hotel accommodations.

Picking a campsite is the vital element in any camping vacation, and it can be every bit as bewildering as choosing the right equipment. Today, you can camp alongside the Grand Canyon, on an Atlantic beach, beside a giant redwood, near mountains, lakes, streams, and meadows. You can even pitch a tent near the mouth of a volcano in Hawaii's Haleakala National Park, or in a

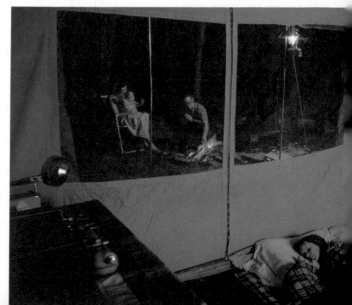

Right: you can pitch a tent in almost any spot —even tucking it right into the rocks for a snug and sheltered site.

Left above: pup tents provide shelter, but they can be cramped. You may have to maneuver to get your boots on and off.

Left: there are large tents roomy enough for the whole family, and even allowing some privacy for Mom and Dad. Even these are compact enough to be convenient.

private campsite in downtown Las Vegas. Campgrounds are either publicly or privately owned, and vary in cost according to the amenities provided. If you're looking for comfort and convenience and plenty of activities for your children, you'll find commercially owned campgrounds a blessing. Most provide electricity and water hookups, sewage and garbage disposal facilities, modern toilets and showers, laundries, food stores, fireplaces, and woodpiles. Some are virtually luxury resorts with swimming pools, golf courses, playgrounds, recreational facilities, restaurants, and even nightclubs. Of course, the more luxuries you demand, the more you have to pay.

What publicly owned campgrounds lack in convenience and luxury they make up for in lower price and natural beauty. Most are situated on large tracts of government land. *Improved* campgrounds are sites that have been especially developed for camping by

Right: good campsites abound in every corner of the USA. This one is nestled in the Catskill Mountains of New York.

Below: if you want to be near the water while camping, you might choose Bahia Honda in Florida.

national, state, and local parks. Here you will find the facilities to be minimal but adequate: a fireplace, picnic table, garbage can, and toilets. The larger and more popular parks often have some of the conveniences found in private campsites. *Unimproved* public campgrounds are precisely that: undeveloped areas that are carefully preserved in their natural state. This is where you will get a glimpse of nature at its most beautiful. Facilities usually consist of no more than a clearing in which you can park your car, and, on rare occasions, a garbage can or

crude fireplace. The rest is pure nature.

Campsites in most national, state, and Canadian public parks are assigned on a first-come, first-served basis, though a limited number of reservations are accepted in the National Park System. Many state parks require reservations, and the more popular sites are usually fully booked up to a year in advance. Camping fees are minimal, ranging from $1 to $5 a night, depending on the facilities available. In the National Park System there is an additional entrance fee of $1 to $3 for use of the park itself. If

you plan to visit several national parks, the Golden Eagle Pass will save you money. It costs about $10, and is valid for one year's free admission to every park in the system. Regulations regarding length of stay, use of fires, and hunting and fishing permits vary from park to park. For detailed information on individual campgrounds, write to state tourist bureaus, or get a copy of *Camping in the National Park System* ($.50) from the U.S. Government Printing Office, Washington, D.C. 20402.

The great increase in the use of public campgrounds has made overcrowding a serious problem in many parks. Unless traffic jams and wall-to-wall people are your idea of a camping vacation, avoid the most popular and highly publicized parks, such as Yellowstone and Yosemite, during the peak summer season and on holiday weekends. Investigate less well-known, but equally beautiful spots such as Bryce Canyon and Canyonlands National Parks, where beautiful campsites often go begging.

What about other public lands controlled by the Department of the Interior? The

National Forest Service is responsible for millions of acres of wooded land and virgin forests, and offers extensive camping facilities for vacationing families. For backcountry campers, the National Wilderness Preservation System, and the Wild and Scenic Rivers Authority, provide pristine camping conditions. But be prepared to rough it. There are no roads or camping facilities, and you must obtain a permit in order to enter.

A comprehensive guide to public and private campgrounds in the United States and Canada will be indispensable in planning your trip. The AAA offers a free *Camping and Trailering Guide* to its members. The best commercial guides are the Rand McNally *Guidebook to Campgrounds*, and Woodall's *Trailer and Camping Guide*. Both describe thousands of different campgrounds, with details on facilities, fees, opening and closing dates, vehicle restrictions, and where to write for additional information or reservations.

If you are an old hand at camping, you are probably already a member of a camping club. If you are a new camper, joining a club is a good idea. Most camping clubs are nonprofit organizations dedicated to encouraging use of the outdoors while protecting and preserving the natural environment. The American Forestry Association (1319 18th St. N.W., Washington, D.C. 20036), Sierra Club (1050 Mills Towers, San Francisco, Calif. 94104), and Wilderness Society (729 15th St. N.W., Washington, D.C. 20005) have nationwide memberships. Being a member entitles you to receive useful and up-to-date information on camping developments, and to participate in a variety of group outdoor activities.

Be realistic about your outdoorsmanship. Extreme climates and unpatrolled areas are for experienced campers only. You would probably feel more comfortable sticking to improved campgrounds, especially if you have small children; but wherever you camp there are rules of safety everyone should follow. Study the area for potential land and water hazards. Keep an eye on your

children. Impossible though it may seem, they can get lost within a few yards of your campsite. Give them a whistle and a mirror when they leave the site so you can find them by the sound of the whistle or flashes of light off the mirror. Adults should carry the same things, plus matches. Never hike alone, and never try to pet or feed wild animals, no matter how sweet or helpless they appear.

Courtesy and consideration are important, too. Keep noise to a minimum, especially at night in crowded campgrounds. Always leave your campsite as clean and litter-free as you found it. Leave trees, flowers, and shrubs undamaged for others to enjoy. Make sure your whole family adopts the old camping motto: "Take nothing but memories. Leave nothing but footsteps.

It is possible to find
unspoiled camping areas
in which you and nature
will be in complete soli-
tude, and you will have
to rely on yourselves.
In other spots, however,
you'll find friendly and
helpful rangers around.

Renting a
Vacation Home

4

Have you ever thought how nice it would be to do *exactly* as you pleased on your vacation? To sleep late or stay outdoors all day if you feel like it; wear whatever you're most comfortable in, day or night; eat whatever you like whenever you're hungry; feel free to socialize or not as the mood takes you; and, best of all, to relax and let the children carry on as usual without worrying that an unexpected tantrum or burst of 6 a.m. exuberance will disturb anyone.

What kind of dream vacation is this? The answer, of course, lies in renting your own vacation house or apartment.

Renting a home like this one in Rhode Island can give you far more freedom than most hotels offer for your vacation accommodation. As you enjoy the typical pastimes and activities of the area, you also get a slant on how people live in other parts of the country, and in other kinds of communities.

It means a bit of fending for yourself, but it also means that you and your family can enjoy a special kind of freedom that's impossible at most hotels. On a vacation in a rented place there are no schedules of mealtimes to be met, and no rules to restrict your youngster's natural high spirits. All are free to do their own thing in their own time, to come and go as they please, and yet

still be together as a family. Renting a vacation home has other advantages, too. By buying your own food and doing your own cooking, you can keep costs within reasonable limits, and still cater to individual tastes and fussy appetites.

Like all dream vacations, however, renting a house has its pitfalls. Your dream can become a nightmare of unwashed dishes, unmade beds, and long hours over a hot stove, and you may wonder why you bothered to leave home. But it doesn't have to work out that way. For one thing, many rented accommodations include daily maid service. Even if your vacation abode doesn't include such a luxury, however, there are other ways

of lightening the domestic load. One of the advantages of this kind of unstructured vacation is that you are not only free of hotel regulations, but also of the routine you usually follow at home. If you're normally a meticulous housekeeper, let yourself relax and live with a little sand and clutter.

There's no need, either, to sit down twice a day to elaborate meals. Take a picnic lunch to the beach, and simply let everybody be responsible for fixing their own midday salad or sandwich. On vacation the whole family is more likely to pitch in with things so everyone can get back to the sun and sea in the shortest possible time. Ordinary chores can actually become part of

vacation you've planned, you'll find a variety of rental accommodations to suit your family's budget and tastes.

How do you go about renting a vacation home? If you're like the majority of American families, you'll probably want to rent in a resort or vacation area you've visited before. Your best bet, then, is to write the local chamber of commerce or regional tourist board for lists of licensed real estate agents specializing in vacation rentals. Many tourist boards can also supply you with a list of inexpensive accommodations for rent—housekeeping cabins, efficiency apartments, etc. If you prefer to find a house on your own, subscribe to a local newspaper, and look through the classified ads.

Once you've found a house that appeals to you, take a day or weekend trip to inspect it. Taking a house sight unseen is a risky

Above: you would have to buy food from a shop like this one if you rented a vacation house in Corfu, Greece. It's a great way to get to know the people.

Right: members of the family are usually more willing to help with cooking, shopping, and household chores in order to insure that all have more leisure.

your vacation fun. If you're accustomed to shopping in large, crowded supermarkets, you'll love browsing through the fresh fruit and vegetables at a local farmers' market, or going down to the docks and buying your fish or lobster right off the boats. If you're vacationing in a foreign country, shopping is a marvelous way to meet the people, and pick up the essence of another way of life.

No matter where you go, or what type of

business. What a glowing advertisement describes as "cozy and rustic" may turn out to be a one-room cabin with no indoor plumbing, and a woodburning stove. "Convenient to shops" could mean your cottage is sandwiched between the local fish market and a Chinese laundry. One family was dismayed to find that their "short walk to the ocean" meant crossing a hazardous four-lane highway. While most advertisers and reputable realtors don't intentionally deceive, the only way you can be absolutely sure what you're getting is to see the house.

If you're renting a cottage at a considerable distance from your home, don't hesitate to ask for a picture of the house, and a detailed description of it and the surrounding area. Are the kitchen and bath-

Where you choose to rent a home or apartment for vacationing depends a lot on what you want to do.

Above left: your choice may be lazing on a beach.

Above: perhaps you are attracted by the simple and quiet pleasures of living in the country.

Left and right: if it's city sightseeing you're after, you might pick Washington, D.C. to see the White House, or San Francisco for Chinatown.

room facilities adequate? Is there heat, or air-conditioning in extreme climates? Are there nearby shops and grocery stores? Will you need a car to get around?

One of the most important things to check before you sign on the dotted line is just how well equipped your vacation house will be. Don't be lulled into a false feeling of security by previous experience. You might find a beach house you rent one year has everything you need—right down to a corkscrew, and ample supply of vintage comic books— while this year's lake cottage has no linen, dishes, or pots and pans. At the very least, checking beforehand will save you the

expense of buying things you could have brought from home.

If you are vacationing far from home, ask your travel agent if you can rent a chalet, villa, or condominium as part of a packaged tour. You can rent a chalet in the Bavarian Alps, for instance, for two weeks, with a free car for the entire length of your stay, for under $850. While a house booked this way is inevitably more expensive than finding one on your own, it is usually fully equipped, and it often comes with fringe benefits that make it more of a bargain.

Renting a vacation home in a popular or fashionable resort area is usually an expensive proposition. One way of keeping costs down, however, is to share a large house with another family. Ideally, this not only saves you money, but it also reduces the number of housekeeping chores because there are more people around to pitch in. On the intangible side, sharing new experiences with old friends can make a vacation more fun for both you and your children.

Even with friends of long standing, however, sharing a home can pose unexpected problems. To begin with, all the children may not get along well. It's difficult for even the closest adult friendships to weather the storms of squabbling offspring. Then, too, if your idea of a relaxing vacation is sleeping until noon, giving a token swipe to housework before dashing to the beach, and partying well into the night, you may belatedly discover that your companions are invariably early risers and meticulous house-

To combine vacation accommodation and transportation, there's nothing like a houseboat's easy operation and hominess. Moving slowly down a river or through a canal on a boat like this can bring you one of the most pleasantly relaxed and refreshing vacations of any you can dream of.

keepers. It helps to consider possible sources of trouble in advance, and come to an agreement about splitting costs, sharing chores, and arranging the children's routine.

If the comfort and convenience of a vacation house appeal to you, but being tied down to one spot does not, try renting a houseboat. These floating homes usually boast all the conveniences of a seaside cottage

—picture windows, carpeted bedrooms, fully equipped kitchens, and baths. With an open space fore and aft for fishing and swimming, and a roof that doubles as a sundeck, you get not only a complete home, but also built-in resort facilities. Best of all, when you get restless, you simply weigh anchor and move on to another mooring, doing your sightseeing from the comfort of your living room sofa. Don't let the intricacies of handling a boat discourage you from trying this unique vacation alternative. There is a saying that "if you can drive a car, you can drive a houseboat." It takes about an hour to understand the controls, which are deliberately kept simple so that vacationers needn't spend half their time poring over an instruction manual. Most rental agencies will give you instruction, well-marked charts and maps, and a trial run before you set out.

Houseboats are ideal for exploring inland waterways, and sheltered coves and islands in intercoastal waters. If you have the time, you might even travel from the St. Lawrence Seaway to the Florida keys, which can be done without once venturing out to sea. At night you pull into a marina, in which slips cost from $1 to $3, tie up near an island, or drop anchor in a secluded cove. Most houseboats accommodate from six to eight people, and cost from $250 to $575 a week—about the cost of a seaside cottage. They come fully equipped with everything you'll need for cruising, except food and gas. For more information write to *Family Houseboating* magazine (Box 2081, Toluca Lake, California 91602) for their *Houseboat Rental Directory;* or to Rent-a-Cruise of America, Florence, Alabama.

Another alternative to renting a traditional vacation house is house swapping—one of the best ideas to come along in years. How would you like to spend a rent-free vacation in a custom-designed home on Cape Cod, a deluxe beach house near Disneyland, a medieval Irish castle beside the river Shannon, a Mexican villa overlooking Acapulco Bay? The only costs to you are transportation and personal expenses. If you're willing

Right: now new vacation homes are designed using the traditional styles but incorporating modern conveniences, as this French development at Port la Galere on the Cote d'Azur, built like a traditional town.

Below: with the increase of tourism on Spain's Costa del Sol, facilities have sprung up for virtually any kind of living arrangements. The pleasant villas shown in our picture are just one example.

Below: in Greece, the old and the new make a harmonious blend to welcome the vacationer. This tranquil harbor scene is at Mykonos, where visitors can rent private rooms overlooking the waterfront.

to exchange your home for someone elses, you can have an economical family vacation anywhere in the world.

How does it work? Last summer Geri and Jim exchanged their Brooklyn Heights apartment for a cottage on the Newfoundland coast. For two weeks they and their three children swam, crewed in a sailboat race, went out on a fishing boat with neighboring islanders, and attended local clambakes. Meanwhile their Canadian friends happily browsed through New York's museums and shops, toured the United Nations, and took in the latest Broadway hits.

This was Jim and Geri's second house swapping experience. The year before they had exchanged homes with an English family, and spent four weeks in a thatched-roof cottage in a small town near Oxford.

When you rent your vacation home, you become a part of a real community. This gives you more of a chance of getting that blend of privacy and socializing you have in your own home—be it a stroll on the beach with your little one, a snooze in the sun on your own, or a huge picnic or chat over drinks with your new and friendly, if only temporary, neighbors.

In their borrowed car they visited London, saw a play at Stratford-upon-Avon, explored the Cotswolds, and toured the ancient colleges of Oxford under the expert guidance of an English don. Best of all, by visiting their neighbors' homes, talking to the local tradesmen, and becoming "regulars" at the local pub, they got to know the English as few ordinary tourists ever do.

House swapping usually works best for people who live at a considerable distance from each other—either in different kinds of climates, or in a different country. Since you

eliminate the cost of accommodation—a major part of any vacation budget—you'll probably find that you can afford to travel farther than you could otherwise. But many people start off by exchanging houses within the same state, and sometimes within the same city, and gradually widen their vacation radius as they become more familiar with the process of home swapping.

How do you go about swapping your home? Until recently the only way to arrange a home exchange was by advertising in a suitable local paper. Now, however, there are several firms that specialize in lists of exchange houses. One of them is the Vacation Exchange Club, Inc., 119 Fifth Avenue, New York, N.Y. 10003. Each spring they publish the *Home Exchange Directory*, which lists thousands of homes offered for exchange all over the world. For a fee of $9.50 they will include a description of your home with information on its amenities, and send you a copy of the *Directory* and two follow-up supplements. Then it's up to you.

All exchanges are made through personal contact between the families involved. They recommend, however, that you choose as many possible trades as you can from the list, and then write to the owners giving details of your own home and family, and requesting similar information from them. Many people include references, photographs, and local tourist information at this stage. Getting to know the other family is an essential part of this type of vacation. It is at the early correspondence stage, too, that you can set up other arrangements. Many families not only swap homes, but also recreational equipment, such as boats, bicycles, and even trailers.

Whatever scheme you choose—to rent or to exchange—you'll soon find that a do-it-yourself vacation offers rewards that cannot be measured purely in terms of cost. Outside the artificial atmosphere of an hotel, you cease being just another tourist. As a real resident, even for a short time, you'll be "at home" wherever you are.

For many people their vacation is the perfect chance to learn a new sport together, laughing at the inevitable mistakes, and taking mutual delight in developing new skills.

Adventure Vacations

5

There was a time when only wealthy sportsmen, fitness fanatics, and confirmed daredevils went on sports vacations, but not any more. The thrills, the glamor, and the adventure remain, but today there are sports vacations to suit every taste and pocketbook. If you've never ridden a horse, paddled a canoe, or sailed a skiff, you're bound to have doubts and questions about active vacations in general. What skills do I need? Must I be a powerhouse of energy? How old must my children be to participate safely? Most outfitters and outdoor organizations will tell you if there is a minimum age or special skill required, and many encourage the participation of children by giving them reduced fees. Some associations, on the other hand, flatly refuse to allow very young children on some

Water is a natural focal point of summer sports.

Left: father and son enjoy a splash in the surf.

Right: sailing fans can charter a craft to sail on their own, or go to a school to learn the skill.

wilderness trips. Their reason is that parents spend so much time minding their offspring that neither parent nor child enjoys the vacation. It's important, when planning for a family adventure, to consider each person's age, physical stamina, and athletic ability.

The water—be it sea, lake, or river—is a natural setting for outdoor vacations. Swimming, of course, is the number one water sport. If you're heading for the water, find out about beginner or refresher courses at your local YMCA, YWCA, or Red Cross. Today there are even programs for "water babies" (three- to four-year-olds), so no one need be left out.

Once you're sure every member of your family is a competent swimmer, you can stop hugging the water's edge, and take a boating vacation. Sailing is one of the most enjoyable sports for families that want to do something together. Skimming across the water in a fresh breeze, and mastering the special skills that go with handling a small craft can give you a marvelous, zestful feeling of freedom. If you and your family have never sailed before, your best bet is to enroll in a sailing

school. At the Annapolis, Md. Sailing School, for example, courses start at $85, with special family reductions. You get 12 hours of instruction, which you can space out over four consecutive weekends, and when you know how to chart a course and trim a sail, you qualify for the vacation cruise course. In this course, you captain your own yacht with family or friends as crew, and sail in a fleet under the supervision of a lead boat. At the Antilles Sailing School in the Virgin Islands, you can charter a 34-foot boat complete with an instructor who sails with you by day, and leaves you safely anchored at night. The yacht has sleeping quarters for up to four people, and costs $600 a week in summer.

If you're already an experienced sailor, you can charter almost any boat that takes your fancy—yawl, ketch, schooner, sloop, motor boat, or cabin cruiser. Depending on the size of the vessel, it will cost you anywhere from $125 to $700 a week. You can even rent a yacht with a captain and crew, if your sailing experience is limited but your budget is not. The average price for a crewed charter

Snorkling is an easy and inexpensive way to explore life under the sea.

Right: scuba diving takes more expertise—and also more money—but it gets you closer to the underwater world, and allows fishing by spear gun.

Below: a group of scuba divers prepare for a day's outing on one of the Caribbean shores.

is $1500 to $3000 a week for six persons.

If sailing a small craft is not for you, and chartering your own yacht won't fit into the family budget, take a windjammer cruise. Windjammer cruises operate out of Maine, Florida, and California. In New England you can explore the irregular coves and picturesque islands of Penobscot Bay, with frequent stops for swimming, visits to old whaling towns, and lobster and clambakes on the beach. Here you will sail by day, and anchor by night. Caribbean skippers cruise the Bahamas, Virgin Islands, and Florida keys, sailing at night to give you more time for beachcombing, water sports, and visiting the small island towns. West Coast windjammers follow the California coastline down to Mexico, putting in at small fishing ports and exotic towns like Puerto Vallarta along the way.

On all windjammers, the stress is on informality and fun. If you wish, you can take a turn at the helm, help hoist the sails, repair rigging, and weigh anchor. Or you can just sit back and soak up the sun and salt air. Most schooners carry between 25 and 65 passengers in cabins that are small but comfortable. On some of the more elaborate vessels you will find air conditioning, wall-to-wall carpeting, and private toilet facilities. The food is plain, homestyle cooking, and there's plenty of it. All-inclusive prices for a windjammer cruise range from $150 to $300 per person. The minimum age on many schooners is 14 to 16.

It's not just the sea's surface that attracts family vacationers. The vast, silent, undersea world is the newest adventure playground. Contrary to popular myth, you don't have to have superhuman strength or courage to explore it. As long as you feel at ease in the water, are in good physical shape, and, for scuba diving, get *professional* training first, there is little danger involved.

Snorkeling, the simplest and most economical type of underwater diving, can be great fun for every member of your family, and is the best introduction to more advanced diving techniques. All you need is a mask, fins, and snorkel, which you can purchase relatively cheaply. Once equipped, you can explore shallow water reefs, and examine underwater life. There is even a nature trail for snorkelers at Buck Island Reef in the Virgin Islands, complete with underwater signs identifying the coral formations.

If you long for the beauties of the seabed, or the chance to explore old shipwrecks, underwater tunnels, and caves, then scuba diving is for you. (Scuba is an acronym for self-contained underwater breathing apparatus.) The basic equipment is an air tank, or aqualung, and regulator. Scuba equipment is expensive to buy, but most instructors and outfitters can rent you everything you will need for a nominal fee, or include it in the cost of instruction. This is one case in which qualified instruction is absolutely essential to your safety. Be sure to find out if your course will lead to certification, a requirement for more advanced dives. You can learn to scuba dive close to home in anything from a YMCA swimming pool to a nearby lake or river—where, by the way, you can examine wrecked boats and machines, observe freshwater marine life, or even hunt for gold. But the dream of most scuba enthusiasts is to dive in the ocean reefs of the Caribbean, where the water is clear and warm, the surf relatively calm, and the underwater life superb.

For as little as $200 you can get special scuba packages to the Caribbean. These include accommodations, meals, instruction, dives, and all your equipment. Your tour might include a dive to a 300-year-old Spanish shipwreck, a treasure hunt, or an underwater photographic safari. Spearfishing, shell collecting, and coral harvesting are discouraged or prohibited because of the damage they do to reefs and underwater life. Many tours combine scuba and snorkeling, thus providing vacation fun for every member of the family, regardless of age or expertise.

Water sports flourish not only on the sea and under it, but also on the millions of miles of inland waterways that crisscross this country. Canoeing is fast becoming the

Above: sailing a small craft is a sporting adventure the whole family can share in. "Hiking out" is one of the skills you will all have to learn in order to keep the boat upright in a stiff wind.

favorite sport of many young families. Why? Not only are canoes the best, and sometimes only, way of exploring wilderness areas, but they are also ideal for one-day and weekend trips closer to home. They are light enough to be "portaged" (carried overland) and to be easily transported by car. In the water they are easy to handle, and surprisingly fast and quiet. Aluminum canoes are the lightest, safest, and easiest to maintain. They range in length from 12 to about 22 feet, and cost from $250 to $400. If you haven't paddled a canoe since your scouting days, or are a complete novice, the best way to judge whether a canoe will suit your family is to rent one by the hour (about $2), day ($7), or week ($30). For a free list of nationwide canoe rental facilities, write to Grumman Boats, Marathon, New York 13803.

If you'd like your first taste of canoeing to be through areas that haven't changed since Indian and early fur trader days, your best bet is to take a guided trip, either through an experienced outfitter, or an outdoor club. Overnight trips include complete camping facilities, food, and all your equipment. A five-day trip with a guide and complete outfitting costs about $150 per person, with special family rates and discounts for children under 16. On some journeys preschoolers ride for free. If you belong to an outdoor club, the cost can be as low as $100 for adults and $60 for children.

Yet another way to get a glimpse of some of this country's most beautiful waterways is to take a float trip. The thought of plunging through thundering rapids in a rubber raft may make you shudder, but most outfitters claim that this is a perfect adventure for every member of your family. The danger is said to be minimal: safety ropes and rails crisscross the raft, every member of your family is equipped with a life jacket, and the entire trip is made under the watchful eyes of an experienced crew and crewmaster. In the Grand Canyon alone, the number of people rafting the white waters of the Colorado River has increased from 55 in 1956 to 15,000 in 1972. In highly publicized

Below: canoeing is gaining popularity as a family sport. Canoes are easy to handle, fast, and quiet —and they provide the best, if not the only, way of exploring wilderness areas on short or long trips.

areas, the government now has to limit the number of rafts allowed on a river in any one year, but there are still hundreds of little known canyons and white water rivers open to family vacationers.

What can you expect? Stretches of glassy, mirrorlike water, alternating with the roar of whirling eddies and rapid currents. All along the way you will stop to swim, picnic, and study the geology and ecology of canyon life. At night you camp at the water's edge, or stay in riverside lodges. The average cost for a five-day trip is $150 to $300 per person, with discounts of as much as 50 per cent for children, sometimes based on weight.

If the very thought of navigating white water sets your head spinning, and the sight of rolling waves makes your stomach churn, then there are countless outdoor vacations to

Above: a farm vacation may provide your children with their first close-up glimpse of cows, horses, and other animals a city dweller may never have seen or felt before.

Above right and right: vacationing on a western ranch means contact with horses, and riding lessons are often given as part of the program.

68

choose from in which you never have to set foot off dry land. "Back to the land" vacations have their own special delights—the smell of freshly turned earth or new-mown hay, the sight of a newborn foal taking its first wobbly steps, the taste of freedom you get from cantering over wide open ranges or blazing your own trail through a tangled wilderness, the sting of the wind on your face as you ski down a snow-covered mountain.

If you have a large family and a limited budget, a visit to a farm or ranch can be a relaxing and economical vacation, especially with very young children. There are more than 500 working farms and ranches through-

Right: another favorite activity for ranch guests is an outdoor barbecue.

out the United States and Canada that take paying guests. Whether you choose a small Wisconsin dairy farm, a 200,000-acre Colorado cattle ranch, or a neat New England fruit and vegetable farm, your family will experience a part of America they may have seen only on television. Accommodations range from a spare room in your host's home to a housekeeping cabin or a luxurious, air-conditioned suite with your own private bath.

On a small farm or ranch you and your children will be treated like friends or relatives. You'll eat with the family, get to know them intimately, and help with simple chores. Your host's children will introduce your own youngsters into the routine of farm life—gathering eggs, feeding animals, and berry picking will keep most children happy and busy for hours on end. Meanwhile you and your husband will have a chance to explore the area—your host can tell you of nearby sights, auctions, summer theaters, etc.—or simply sit and relax. The whole family will be invited to meet the neighbors, and attend local picnics, square dances, or county fairs. The larger the farm, the more

activities you will have to choose from. Many are now equipped with swimming pools, well-stocked trout ponds, and tennis and other sports facilities.

Western ranches, of course, have their own special attraction. The emphasis, naturally, is on horses, and you'll find that most ranches include riding instruction in the cost of your vacation. As your riding skill improves, and your bottom adjusts to long periods of time in the saddle, you might venture out on an overnight pack trip. The extra cost, about $10 per person, is minimal compared to the fee for nonguests, which can be as high as $60 a day. Most ranches and outfitters that specialize in this type of activity are heavily concentrated in the Rocky Mountain area—

Colorado, Utah, Wyoming, Idaho, and Montana. The mountain trails will take you through spectacular terrain and remote alpine meadows, along sparkling streams, and through virgin forests. The ride is usually taken in easy stages, to give you time to take pictures, hike, or just lie on your back and enjoy being, literally, on top of the world. There are good camps and good food at the end of each day's ride.

If you're an experienced rider you can join in the traditional ranch work—rounding up cattle, riding fence, or going on a seasonal cattle drive. Though cattle are no longer driven to market, many ranches still move their herds to new pastures every spring, summer, and fall. To most, the two- to four-day drives make us as authentic "cowboys" as we would ever hope to be. You ride with the cowpunchers, help chase strays, eat from the back of a chuckwagon—which nowadays is often a truck—and sleep under the stars. It's hot, dusty work. You rise at dawn, and spend close to 12 hours in the saddle. While it's an experience for none but the most skilled riders, it is a rare experience, and one you and your family will long remember.

There's another way of seeing the west from the vantage point of an early pioneer, but this way doesn't involve long hours in the saddle: a trip in a covered wagon. Although some ranches keep wagons for their guests, the two big covered wagon outfitters are Wagons Ho in Kansas, and Wagons West in Wyoming. Both firms try to duplicate the pioneer's experience in every detail, with the addition, however, of some modern comforts like foam-covered seats and rubber wheels. You follow the same prairie trails that the Mormons and other early settlers used, and in some places you can still see the rut marks from a hundred years ago. You eat fresh meat and vegetables cooked over an open fire, and sleep under the stars, or in your wagon. There's even a real-life Cheyenne Indian raid to recreate that bit of pioneering history.

The only modern vehicle that dares to go places where horses and wagons once did is the four-wheel-drive jeep. If you think a jeep ride is a soft way to explore the wilderness, however, you're in for a surprise. Bouncing around in a jeep, and holding on for dear life might make you glad to get back to a comfortable saddle. But the jeep is perfect for making long trips to remote spots in the shortest possible time. Some ranches include overnight and daylong jeep trips in their weekly rates. They use them for excursions to ghost towns, abandoned gold mines, and ancient Indian monuments and burial grounds. For longer trips into the wilderness you can hire your own vehicle and guide, or join a caravan. Navigating rugged, unmarked terrain can prove a difficult chore for a novice, so if you've never driven a jeep

To get a small taste of how pioneers might have fared going West in the last century, take a trip on an old-fashioned wagon train. Wagons today will often have rubber tires to give you a smoother ride, but in many other respects, the trip will duplicate the experiences of the fearless pioneers.

before, you'd be wise to stick to a guide and driver. The cost is about $25 a day per person, with special rates for children and family groups.

What else does a ranch vacation offer? In addition to hours of horseback riding and special side trips, you can dance at hoedowns, enjoy delicious barbecues, take a romantic, moonlight hayride, or watch an old-time rodeo. The cost of a farm or ranch vacation, with meals included, ranges from $50 to $160 a week for an adult, and approximately half that for a child. For detailed information on costs, locations, and activities at hundreds of farms and ranches throughout the country, write for a copy of *Farm and Countryside Ranch Guide* ($3.50), published by Adventure Guides, Inc., 36 East 57th Street, New York, N.Y. 10022.

Of course, summer isn't the only time you and your family can take an outdoor vacation, nor are rugged trips into the wilderness the only way to combine adventure with family fun. If you prefer the flair and the conviviality of resort life, why not try skiing this winter? Few other sports offer as much fun for every member of the family—whether a toddler who is just beginning to walk, a teenager out to break Olympic records, or a slightly overweight, underconditioned husband. Today's resorts provide ski slopes for every level of proficiency. There is no doubt that skiing is expensive, especially if you have to travel far to reach the slopes, and invest in equipment for your whole family. Skis, poles, boots, and clothes can run from $1500 to $2000 for a family of four. Even renting your equipment, when combined with the cost of chairlifts (often a whopping $10 a

day), instruction, accommodation, and meals, can run into a good deal of money. Nevertheless, if you plan carefully, a skiing vacation doesn't have to be beyond your reach.

Probably the cheapest type of ski holiday is a five- to seven-day "learn to ski" package, offered by most resorts, and many airlines. The package usually includes transportation, accommodation, lifts, ski school, and sometimes meals. Consult your travel agent, and shop around for the package best suited to your family's needs. If you're going it alone, you'll save money by renting your equipment from a ski shop near home rather than waiting till you arrive at a resort. The typical rate for skis, boots, and poles on the slopes is $8 to $10; at home, $4 to $6. When visiting your local shop, check to see if it sponsors its own ski tours to nearby resorts. In many cases, a shop can not only rent you equipment, but also provide transportation and

group rates at some popular ski resorts.

Avoid high fashion ski shops. Dressing your family for the slopes needn't cost you an arm and a leg. Most young children can wear their everyday snowsuits with a heavy sweater underneath. Older children and adults will need waterproof ski parkas and a pair of stretch ski pants, which are often cheaper at big department stores. Heavy sweaters, woolen hats and mittens, and warm underwear—tights, "long johns," or a body stocking—are probably already a part of your family's winter wardrobe. If you simply must have something fashionable, then keep your eyes open for end-of-the-winter sales, when the cost of ski apparel is often halved. However else you budget, don't try to save by skipping ski lessons; proper instruction could make or break your vacation. Almost every resort has a ski school.

If your budget just won't stretch enough to meet the high costs of a resort, there is another type of skiing that is growing in popularity. Cross-country, or ski touring, which originated in Norway, is much gentler and much cheaper than downhill skiing. For cross-country skiing you use different skis and equipment, which rent for about $5 a day, and you save ski lift charges because ski

Left: a skier stands poised to begin her run, and, in that moment, is filled with a magnificent sense of freedom that is the essence of a winter vacation in the mountains. The view is part of the enjoyment. Below: a skiing class goes through the paces of learning the kick turn. Skiing uses muscles differently from the normal run of daily activities, and it is important for the novice skier to get proper instruction to ensure both pleasure and safety.

lifts aren't needed. For a small membership fee in the Stowe Cross-country Ski Club, and no further charge, you can use more than 40 miles of trails at the Trapp Family Lodge in Vermont.

How does ski touring work? You push, glide, and slide your way, at your own pace through a snow-covered world. You can follow established paths, or set out across fields and woods on your own. The Adirondack Mountain Club in New York maintains

Left: in snowbound country, snowmobiles can be a means of transportation as well as of recreation.

Above: starting a run down from the top is one of the most exciting moments in skiing, especially with such a great view.

what is probably the most extensive system of ski touring trails in the East, some of which lead to winter camps with sleeping and cooking facilities. For a *Ski Touring Guide* ($1.50) of east coast trails, and information on equipment and techniques, write to the Ski Touring Council, West Hill Road, Troy, Vermont 05868 You can ski tour in many national parks all over the country (take note: they are often unbearably crowded in the summer), and in remote areas where you can visit ghost towns and ice-locked lakes, and spend the night in alpine huts or snow camps.

Most of the vacation ideas suggested in this chapter can be arranged independently. Lists of private outfitters, costs, and services can be found in the *Adventure Trip Guide* ($2.95), published by the same firm that produces *Farm, Ranch and Countryside Guide* (Adventure Guides, Inc., 36 East 57th St., New York, N.Y. 10022). If you prefer exploring the wilderness with others who share your interests, your best solution is to join an outdoor club. Nonprofit organizations like the American Forestry Association, American Youth Hostels, Inc., Sierra Club, Wilderness Association, and Appalachian Mountain Club have special family memberships, and sponsor year-round outdoor activities, often at a price well below individual rates.

Finally, in planning any outdoor trip, you'll usually discover that the majority of professional guides and tour organizers believe active vacations are family affairs—adventures that bridge the generation gap, and unite your family in an experience to remember.

Vacations to Stretch the Mind
6

On a broad river, in a flowering orchard, inside a museum—all these locations, and others still, can be a kind of classroom for an educational vacation. The old maxim that learning can be fun is proved by the many who now use vacations to broaden their horizons.

Do you sometimes want more from a vacation than a suntan and a pile of picture postcards? More and more families are using their leisure time not just for relaxation, but also for self-improvement, education, and cultural enrichment. The old saying that "education never ends" is true for many people in many ways. Every year thousands of adults attend continuing education courses—sometimes for credit, sometimes just for fun, and sometimes for inspiration. Educational vacations are more popular today than ever before.

In case you think learning has to be a dull classroom experience, consider some of the courses offered in some university summer sessions. You can study hot air balloon riding or Eskimo beadwork, learn to folk dance or speak any language from French to Swahili, visit behind the scenes at the British Broadcasting Corporation or the kitchen of a great Paris restaurant, take a photographic safari to Africa or study the fauna of Alabama, dig up a dinosaur or a prehistoric civilization, learn how to climb a mountain, sail a boat, or scuba dive. All for university credit! Most of these courses, as well as the more traditional studies, have no prerequisites, and many welcome whole families; but the best part of these educational happenings is that learning no longer takes place in a stuffy classroom. Field trips, tours abroad, and study in the outdoors have become the trademark of summer learning.

Universities and private educational centers around the country also provide exciting learning experiences in resort-type settings at prices well below the more traditional vacation resorts. At Drew Uni-

versity in New Jersey, for example, you can spend a week attending lectures and seminars on anything from modern art to philosophy, films, and politics. Between classes you can swim, take long nature hikes, and even attend the New Jersey Shakespeare Festival on campus. The total cost for meals and lodging is only $175 per person. Stonehill College in Massachusetts offers "spacious campus facil-

ities for creative leisure time", as well as recreational facilities, historical and cultural tours, and reasonable rates.

Many families use their vacation time to learn an art or craft they can then pursue all year round. There are several private and university-sponsored workshops in which would-be artists and potters can find instruction and inspiration. At the Idyllwild School

its low-priced instruction in drawing, painting, and other arts, all you have to do is pile your family into a camper and park nearby. The University of Wisconsin's Indianhead Area Arts Center at Shell Lake offers fascinating workshops in textile design, printmaking and tie-dye work for as little as $70 per person, including tuition, room, and board.

How do you find out about university travel programs and summer courses? Write to the adult education or summer session office at nearby state universities, or send for the current edition of James Treloar's book, *Educational Vacations* ($5.95), a directory of outdoor and foreign travel courses offered by American universities. It is available from Gale Research Company, Book Tower, Detroit, Michigan 48226. Publications in Continuing Education, 105 Roney Lane, Syracuse, New York 13210, can also advise you on year-round educational opportunities that can be adapted to vacation study.

What about planning your own cultural vacation? If you're a music loving family, but rarely find time to indulge your interest during the year, there are music festivals across the country and around the world that make marvelous holiday destinations. Many of them, like the well-known Berkshire Festival at Tanglewood, Mass., and the Aspen Festival in Colorado, feature major conductors and soloists, and the quality of the music is as good as you would find in the best concert hall. Some festivals serve as the summer residences for major orchestras—Tanglewood is the summer home for the Boston Symphony, Saratoga Springs, N.Y. for the Philadelphia Orchestra, Ravinia for

of Music and Art in Southern California you can study painting, ceramics, music, or dance in a spectacular mountain setting. There are special classes for children, and plenty of recreational activities to keep the whole family happy between classes. Every summer the University of Idaho sponsors an art workshop on wheels at different scenic locations in the state. To take advantage of

Left and right: there are many programs that give you the opportunity to participate in music making, whether you already play an instrument, or want to learn how to.

Below: both indoors and out, music festivals abound in all parts of the country during the summer. They can be enjoyed by the whole family.

the Chicago Symphony, and the Hollywood Bowl for the Los Angeles Philharmonic. What makes music festivals even more enchanting to vacationers are their magnificent natural settings. Tanglewood offers some of the most beautiful and peaceful scenery in Massachusetts. Aspen is as noted for its soaring mountains as for its fine music. The Grand Teton Festival at Jackson Hole, Wyoming, probably commands the most glorious spot of all. Others are set on princely estates—like Caramoor, a baronial mansion with 150 landscaped acres of lawns, gardens, and woodland only 40 miles from New York City.

Tickets to summer music festivals are usually well below the price of those for the same quality performances in a big city, and most festivals have even lower general admission prices—you can bring a blanket, a picnic dinner and a bottle of wine, and lounge on the lawn while listening to the performance. Be warned, however, that most good festivals are sold out well in advance, so buy your tickets early. If your taste is varied (or your children's isn't), many festivals combine classical music with pop, rock, folk, and jazz. At Ravinia, for instance, you can hear Mozart on Friday night and Judy

Collins on Saturday. So it's sometimes possible to interest every member of your family, regardless of age, in a music-oriented vacation.

If you're planning a trip abroad, don't neglect to find out what festivals will be held while you are there. European music events have their own special flavor, and are often held in fine, old buildings, or on important historic sites. For instance, you can hear a Handel opera in Salisbury Cathedral, devotional music in the awesome abbey of Mont St. Michel, outdoor opera in romantic Verona, or Verdi's *Aida* in the Roman Baths of Caracalla.

If it's stage shows you're after, whether *Hamlet* or *Hello Dolly*, plan your vacation along the strawhat circuit. Here you can see

Left: the summer entertainment scene usually includes ballet as well as other kinds of dance.

Right: theater often moves outdoors for the summer. Here is an example of a play given in the grounds of New York City's Cloisters.

all-time favorite shows and star-studded Broadway hits without having to venture into New York. Not all summer theater productions are New York hand-me-downs, either. Keep your eyes open for new plays by unknown playwrights. (Neil Simon, the famous Broadway and Hollywood writer, got his first break in a small playhouse in Buck's County, Pennsylvania.) Every summer, the Eugene O'Neill Memorial Theater in Waterford, Connecticut sponsors a playwright's conference during which you can see the works of young writers produced by professional actors and directors. If you're lucky, you might be in on the discovery of a new O'Neill.

If you're a theater buff, you probably already know that excellent Shakespeare productions are presented in an out-of-the-way Canadian town called, suitably enough, Stratford, Ontario. The works here are often said to rival those staged in the bard's hometown in England. Two additional theaters in Canada's Stratford offer new and unfamiliar plays, midweek musical events, and a major film festival. This means that you can spend a week in the Stratford area, and see something different every night. Shakespearean companies can be found all across the USA as well. In Ashford, Oregon the plays are performed as they were in Elizabethan times—in traditional costume and without intermissions. Other famous Shakespeare sites: Stratford, Connecticut; Carmel-by-the-Sea, California, and New York City's Central Park, where you see the

You can learn many an interesting thing without ever cracking a book on educational vacations. How about an archeological dig? The work is hard but rewarding. For the more athletic and daring, how about a mountain climbing or cave exploring course?

plays free during the summer months.

A complete list of summer theaters would be too long to include here. You can travel from California to Cape Cod visiting a new theater each night. Check with state tourist bureaus for lists of theaters, music festivals, and other cultural events held during the summer months.

If your children are older, an unusual and rewarding vacation idea is to participate in an archeological dig. Until recently, excavating was an activity reserved for scholars; but today, more and more digs train amateurs in exchange for their voluntary labor. If you're not afraid of hard work or dirt, then this is your chance to learn the principles of field archeology while seeing the past unfold before your eyes. Depending where you excavate, you may be set to work digging, washing shards and other artifacts, cataloging and numbering finds, or doing restoration work. If you have a particular skill, such as architectural or mechanical drawing, you'll be particularly welcome on digs.

Most universities sponsor their own digs, and offer inclusive field trips during the summer months. They can be expensive, however, often running over $1000 for transportation, room and board, and tuition. Duke University in North Carolina, for example, sponsors a dig at a Roman site in Israel. Participants live in A-frame houses, share communal meals, and learn all aspects of field archeology for a fee of $350, exclusive of transportation. On the other hand, if you are visiting Israel, and would like to work on a site sponsored by the Israeli government, your room and board for two weeks could be

Right: many tours abroad are designed to appeal to the history buff. This one is in Paestum, Italy.

Below: even university summer courses are often informally out of doors.

as low as $52. You won't get the same type of instruction, but you'll still learn a lot.

There are other archeological sites throughout Europe which are inexpensive if you are willing to arrange your own transportation and accommodation. At Avenche in Switzerland, for example, you can spend three weeks digging among the fascinating remains of Aventicum, capital of Roman Switzerland. You get on-the-spot training in digging, restoration, and draftsmanship, rooms at a small chalet, and meals in a local restaurant at no cost to you except transportation. England, too, offers many opportunities for amateur archeologists. You can excavate the remains of an early Roman villa at St. Albans, help record and catalog prehistoric finds in Norwich, or dig at a medieval site in

York. There is no fee at any of these sites, but you must commit yourself to a minimum stay of two weeks. At York you will even be paid the princely sum of $3.75 for each day's labor.

Many universities sponsor digs closer to home at reasonable costs. You can take your family to Arizona to dig among Indian ruins, or excavate prehistoric sites in Maine and Appalachia. Idaho State University operates three digs within the state, and welcomes families with young children—though only adults can dig. Tents, meals, cots, and tuition cost about $120 per student. For more information on university-sponsored digs, both at home and abroad, contact universities directly. If you are interested in working at an overseas archeological site, write to the

national tourist bureau of the country you want to visit. Another good source of information on archeological sites around the world is Educational Expeditions International, 68 Leonard Street, Belmont, Massachusetts.

While shopping around for educational vacations designed to suit your family, you might discover your teenager has definite ideas of his own. Since so many study trips and courses are designed for young people, the question, "Why can't I do something on my own?" may well be asked. Perhaps the moment has arrived to answer, "Why not?" Sooner or later every youngster goes his or her own way at vacation time, and educational or work holidays, with their built-in supervision, are often the best way of

bridging the gap between sheltered family travel, and total independence. If you'd like more information on work, study, and travel opportunities specifically for students, get in touch with the Council on International Educational Exchange, 777 United Nations Plaza, New York, N.Y. 10017. They publish an excellent guide, *The Whole World Handbook*, and will also give your teenager information on student discounts, charter flights, and low-cost tours.

Combining relaxation with learning— whether it's a new idea, a new interest, or a new skill—can be every bit as exciting as shooting the rapids. It can also add a new dimension to your vacation time, and one that will last a long time after your suntan has disappeared.

Once-in-a-Lifetime Vacations

7

So this is the year you and your family are going to take that once-in-a-lifetime vacation. Perhaps it's a trip to Europe or a Caribbean cruise, a cross-country tour or a visit to an exotic island. Whatever your destination, you've probably been saving and dreaming of this vacation for years. Suddenly, mixed in with the excitement and thrills, are the problems of translating fantastic travel dreams into reality. How do you begin? This chapter can't hope to answer all your questions, but it does offer plenty of practical advice and hints on some of the more common travel headaches —from getting a passport to choosing a packaged tour, to tipping on a cruise ship, to making some sense out of the different air fares.

Let's begin with how you're going to get where you want to go. Long-distance air fares are one of the few commodities that has actually come down in price during the past few years. In 1960, for example, the cheapest fare from New York to London was $350. Today the typical fare on the same route is $256. On both domestic and international routes, airlines offer a bewildering variety of discount fares. Before buying your plane ticket, shop around for the best air fare bargain for your family. Here are some common discount fares on the domestic scene: *excursion fare* offers a 25 per cent discount if you stay a minimum of seven days, and fly midweek. It is applicable only on flights of 1500 miles or more. *Night coach rates* give a 25 per cent discount for traveling outside the peak hours. The newest domestic bargain is the *advanced scheduled flight*, which applies only to long distance routes. By booking your flight three months in advance, making a non-refundable 10 per cent deposit when you reserve, and paying the balance one month before departure, this plan saves you a whopping 46 per cent over the normal coach fare.

Air fare bargains become even more complicated when you're flying abroad. The International Air Transport Association (IATA) regulates all overseas fares with constantly changing rules that are almost incomprehensible to the layman. It's worth the effort, however, of sorting out the major bargains before booking your flight. On the 21- to-45-day *excursion fares*, you must remain for a minimum number of days, and return within a prescribed period. The *individual tour basing fare* (ITX) has a 14- to-21-day stay requirement and also requires that you pay $70 per person in advance for land arrangements. The *group inclusive tour* (CIT) has the same restrictions as the ITX, but also requires that you travel and return with a group of at least 15 people. The *bulk inclusive tour* (BLT) is the cheapest commercial transatlantic airfare, and applies to any group of 40 people who put down a 25 per cent nonrefundable deposit three months before departure, and pay the remainder of the charter fare in full 60 days before departure. Don't let the group requirement put you off. The group is

A rainy day in London doesn't deter the intrepid tourist from watching—and enjoying—the colorful pageantry of the changing of the guards at Buckingham Palace. This is one of the most popular attractions of a city that is especially attractive to Americans because of our historical link.

Most visitors to Paris get to the Louvre to see the *Mona Lisa,* probably one of the most viewed pictures in the world.

formed by the airline, which merely lumps together 15 or 40 people whose arrival and departure dates are the same.

Confused? Try adding a welter of major and minor restrictions and price differentials—like the day of the week you travel, the time of day and the time of year. Then be warned that every fare and discount plan is subject to instant revision or cancellation at the whim of IATA or the Civil Aeronautics Board (CAB). Only a professional can begin to sort out all the problems, and tell you what current fares represent the best travel bargain for your family.

Which brings us to a vital step in planning your trip—a visit to your local travel agent. A travel agent is a trained professional who can advise you on the best and cheapest way to travel, make all your reservations, and help plan your itinerary. His fees are paid by the companies who get your business through him, not by you. Your agent can charge you for transatlantic calls and cables, but he should tell you in advance.

Unfortunately, there are more than a few travel agents who are more concerned with their own profits than your family's travel needs. If you feel you are being pressured into spending more than you wish, or going places you don't want to, don't hesitate to change agents in midstream—and be sure to report the culprit to the American Society of Travel Agents. The travel agent makes extra money only if he manages to book you into hotels that give him a cut of the profits, so he will naturally attempt to steer you to these hotels. Don't let him steer you to hotels you don't like or can't afford.

One of the first questions a travel agent will ask you is whether you want to travel independently, or on a package tour. Whether your destination is Lisbon or Las Vegas, it's safe to say that you will get the most for your money by taking a package tour. Why? Because tour operators are able to make huge advance bulk bookings for airplane seats and hotel beds. By promising to fill those seats and beds for a long period

The distinctive and characteristic sights of various countries you visit will become rich additions to your vacation memories—and make you want to go back again.

These are some of the memory-makers for the European traveler (going counterclockwise) : London's Tower Bridge; wine tasting in France, perhaps in a Loire chateau like the one pictured; Rome's ancient Appian Way; Brussel's Grand Place; and a chalet on the water in Austria.

of time, they can negotiate extremely low rates—a benefit that is passed on to you in more reasonable rates.

A package tour doesn't have to be stifling. Today, tours stress freedom and flexibility as much as economy and convenience. You can travel alone or with a group, sightsee on your own or with a guide, stay at the hotel of your choice, pick your own means of transportation, and sometimes choose your own restaurants. There are two types of packages—the escorted or group tour, and the independent or economy package. If you prefer traveling with others, and don't want to have to cope with troublesome arrangements like schedules, transfers, and baggage, then an escorted tour is for you. Throughout the trip you will be accompanied by a guide who will not only serve as troubleshooter and interpreter, but will also tell you a good deal about the places you visit. Since an escorted tour is usually fully paid in advance, sometimes right down to the tips, you have the added advantage of knowing exactly what your vacation will cost before you set out. If you're more adventurous, you'll find the independent package tour offers the most flexibility, while still providing group rates on round-trip transportation and other major arrangements (car rental, hotel accommodation, transfers, sightseeing, and some meals). Although you must meet specific arrival and departure dates, usually you are free to go where you want, and see what you want.

Nowadays the variety of package tours is almost boundless. You can take a cooking tour of Paris, or learn how to play soccer in England; visit Dracula's land in Romania, or go birdwatching in the Galapagos; spend a week on a houseboat in Venice, or live in a chalet in Austria. It all depends on your tastes and budget. A new development on the package scene is the combination tour. Fly/drive tours have become increasingly popular at home and abroad, giving you the speed of jet travel along with the freedom of your own car. One tour will fly a family of

Above: nothing seems more evocative of Spain than the traditional bullfight (top) and the equally traditional but more lighthearted Flamenco dancing (bottom). Spain's sunny summer is a draw, too.

Left: the cultural and historical richness of Rome has a never-ending fascination for tourists, especially those from younger nations such as ours, and has earned it the name of "the eternal city". Whether fountain, people, or ancient monuments, there's an inviting snapshot everywhere you look.

95

A Caribbean cruise can give you a luxurious dose of sun on shipboard, and interesting stops at such sunny islands as Bermuda.

four to California, and give them a car for a week for less than $500. A "week on wheels" tour to Holland includes round-trip airfare, a rented car with unlimited mileage, two night's accommodation, and many other bonuses for about $314 per person. Fly/cruise packages will jet you to Florida, where you board a liner for a full seven days of cruising in the warm waters of the Caribbean. Airfare and cruise together can cost as low as $295. Other packages combine jet travel with rail and bus transport, use of fully equipped campers, and, in some cases, bicycles.

Of course, not all tours start and end in an airport. If you're deathly afraid of flying, or feel you'll miss too much by staying above the clouds, there are many earthbound packages to choose from. A perennial favorite with travelers is the bus tour—and with good reason. On a bus you can sit back and let the scenery come to you, with none of the frustrations of driving. Today most tour buses are luxury vehicles with air-conditioning, panoramic windows, reclining seats, rest rooms, and even bars and lounges. Greyhound and Continental Trailways, among others, offer an amazing variety of escorted tours throughout the length and breadth of North America.

Rail tours are another leisurely alternative to air travel. Since 1971 when Congress established Amtrack, America's first nationwide passenger rail system, railroads have improved greatly. Spotless dining cars serving fine food, luxurious lounges, and dome cars for relaxation and sightseeing, comfortable reclining chairs, and a choice of sleeping car accommodations allow you to enjoy old-fashioned train travel in new-style comfort. Amtrack offers a variety of tours, from weekend "city getaways" (for as low as $29) to a 10-day New Mexico Adventour for $317, and a Florida "week on wheels" package in which a rental car is included in your rail fare for $259. (These costs are based on a family of four traveling from New York City.)

The most elegant of package tours, and for

Right: letting someone else do the driving is one of the biggest appeals of bus tours—plus the fact that new tour buses are now so comfortable and well equipped. This tour is to the nation's capital.

Right: modern trains are better than they have been in years. Many provide special cars that give a wide and full view of the passing landscape.

many of us the ultimate in luxurious relaxation, is a pleasure cruise. Once considered the domain of the idle rich and retired couples, cruise ships have undergone a dramatic renaissance. Today, low prices and special family rates, shorter cruises, year-round warm water sailings, and exciting novelty packages, attract passengers of all ages and incomes. A typical seven-day cruise from New York to the Caribbean costs from $250 to $750 per person. The lower rate is for minimum accommodation (an inside cabin on a lower deck), which is usually booked early, and is not always available. Outside staterooms are more expensive. Since you'll spend most of your time in the public part of the ship (there is only one class on cruise ships, so you eat the same food and hear the same music no matter what you pay), you can safely take the cheapest cabin that will hold your family. If your children are under 12 they can sail at half fare when sharing a room with you. At least one line (Cunard) has introduced special family rates on its summer cruises. Two adults paying full fare can take along one child under 12 free, others under 12 for $50 each, and children 12 to 18 for half fare.

What do you get for your money? In addition to all the facilities of a first class resort (swimming pool, sauna, gym, etc.), you have your pick of nightly entertainment in a variety of nightclubs and discotheques. You will dine like royalty—cruise food is invariably good and plentiful.

The ship also serves as your hotel when you call at ports. Everything is included in your base fare, except for drinks, personal expenditures, and tips. How do you tip on a cruise ship? It's really not as complicated as it's made out to be, and is no more expensive than tipping in a hotel. On a cruise, you don't give tips until the night before you dock. The two people who will render you the most service are your room steward and table steward. You should divide at least four per cent of your ticket fare between them, adding a further 25 per cent of this sum for each additional member of your family. Another way to figure the tip is on the basis of $1 to $2 per day, per couple, and another 25 per cent for each additional member of your family. Smaller sums, totaling one or two per cent of your fare, can be distributed to other stewards who have served you (deck, night, or wine steward). Special services might warrant an increase. Put the money in a special envelope, and distribute it after dinner on the last night of your cruise.

What should you look out for when picking a package tour? First be warned that the sensationally inviting price in big print at the top of a tour brochure is the lowest. It probably indicates the rate for midweek departure in the off-season. Peak season prices may be twice as high, and you may have to pay surcharges for weekend departures, single rooms, and day flights. Then, too, the lowest price usually means you get minimal accommodation—perhaps a room without bath in a guesthouse, or in a small resort with no swimming or sport facilities. Be sure to check carefully, also, what meals are included in your package. Many tours at rock bottom prices frankly offer no meals at all, or breakfast only. On other packages, "dine around" plans are featured options

which are clearly over and above the basic cost of the tour. Watch out for the tour that includes three meals a day in one city, and none in the next, and that buries information somewhere in a complicated itinerary. Food is an expensive part of any vacation, and must be budgeted for in advance if it is not included in the tour price. If you decide at the outset to go it alone, then budgeting will be one of your principal concerns. There are many travel guides that give clear and up-to-date advice to the budget-conscious independent traveler. In this chapter, we can list only a few of the major bargains available.

If you're planning an extensive cross-country trip, both Greyhound and Continental Trailways offer discount passes valid for unlimited travel throughout the USA and Canada. The one month pass costs $149 (or two months for only $50 more).

Going abroad? Even if you fly the Atlantic, you will still have to solve the problem of ground travel once you reach Europe. If you plan to cover many miles, and you'd like to travel as the Europeans do, there is no better means of going than by rail. There is also no better travel buy than the Eurail pass. Only residents of North and South America can obtain one, and the pass must

Right: no one who goes to the alluring islands of Hawaii wants to miss the fun and good eating of a traditional luau.

Below: these lucky tourists are in Hawaii during Aloha Week, an exciting and festive yearly event.

be purchased *before* you leave home. The Eurail pass is good for unlimited first class travel on the railways of 13 countries (not including Britain, which has its own Thrift Rail Pass), and also on designated lake and river steamers, bus routes, and ferries. The cost for a 21-day pass is $140; one month, $175; and two months, $245. Children 4 to 12 ride at half fare. The quality of European trains is superb. They are clean and comfortable, run frequently, and are usually on time. The crack Trans European Expresses, which connect major cities in nine countries, will whisk you to your destination in high-speed luxury. The motor equivalent of the Eurail pass is the Eurobus pass, issued by Europabus, a vast network of international bus lines covering more than 70,000 miles. Europabus also offers a wide selection of individual tours at bargain prices. For instance, a five-day, all-inclusive tour of ancient Greece, leaving from Athens, costs less than $100.

If you're traveling independently, you can save dollars by waiting until you cross the Atlantic to make your tour arrangements. England and Denmark offer the best buys in tours to all parts of Europe, the Middle East, and North Africa. Just go to a travel agent after you arrive, and find out what's available. Besides saving money, you'll see Europe in the company of Europeans rather than with a bus load of your

101

own compatriots. This can give you an interesting slant on things.

Accommodation is your next problem, or challenge, depending on your point of view. If you'll be in Europe during the crowded summer months, it's wise to make hotel arrangements before you arrive. Your travel agent can help you with this; but if you're planning to stay in budget hotels, you'll probably have to do most of the work yourself. Again, there are scores of guides that list low-cost accommodation all over Europe. (Fielding's is one of the best). Should you happen to arrive in a city without a reservation, most train stations have an

which is obtainable from consulates or travel agents. For all other foreign travel you will need a passport. If you've never had a passport before, you must apply in person to a State Department Passport agency; a clerk of a federal, state or probate court; or a postal clerk designated by the Postmaster General. Take with you proof of U.S. citizenship (birth, baptismal, or naturalization certificate); identification with your signature and description on it (such as a driver's license); and two recent passport photos. Birth certificates must be official and validated. Vending machine pictures are not acceptable. It's better to go to a professional

Though Mexico is our nearest neighbor, it's culture is much different. This, combined with a generally good climate, makes it as inviting a spot to visit as many a far distant place. Left: Diego Rivera's strong murals deal with themes of the people. Above and right: handicrafts for sale.

accommodation bureau, which, for a small fee, will find you a room—and usually at the price you want to pay.

When you book a tour or flight outside the United States, your travel agent will tell you what tourist documents are required. For trips to Canada, Mexico, and the Caribbean, you will only need proof of citizenship (a driver's license, voter's registration, or birth certificate), and in some cases a tourist card,

photographer who knows the required size and pose. For a fee of $12 you'll be issued a passport valid for five years. If your children are very young, you'll probably want to have them included on your passport. While family passports are available (for husbands, wives, and all dependent children under 18), they severely restrict individual travel rights. Allow a minimum of two or three weeks for your passport to be processed, especially if

102

you are traveling in the peak summer season. If you're traveling outside Western Europe or South America, you will probably need a visa—official permission to visit a country granted by the government of that country. Your travel agent will tell you if you need one, and can obtain it for you for a small charge.

Once you have your passport and your cruise, rail, or airplane ticket, you're ready to go—except for the thousand other things left to be done (like brushing up on your high school Spanish, reading one or two guidebooks, shopping and packing for yourself and your family). Planning and preparing for a once-in-a-lifetime vacation can be a full-time job, but one that has a built-in reward—the vacation itself. You might even find that once-in-a-lifetime just isn't often enough, and go for more.

Weekends should not slip by either unnoticed or unappreciated, because these two days can provide a welcome break from the weekday routine. There's usually plenty to do and see if you just take the time and the little bit of effort it needs to plan something. Whether it's a special event—such as a parade or big baseball game— or do-it-yourself activi- ties—such as hiking, biking, or playing a game—you should make the most of weekends for family fun and recreation.

104

Weekend Wanderings
8

The funny thing about weekends is that they always seem to be ending. There's always another one around the corner, of course, but before you know it, it too has come and gone just like the rest. More often than not, we let our two free days a week go by without doing anything to make them memorable and special. Weekends are really mini-vacations, and once you begin to think of them that way, you'll realize that, just like their longer counterparts, they must be planned with care if they're to become happy family memories.

Many of the ideas in this book can be adapted to weekend trips. You can camp overnight in a nearby park or by the seashore, canoe on a local river or lake, sign up for a sailing or skiing weekend package, attend a play or concert, take a course, spend two days cruising the Caribbean, or even exchange your home with another family in a nearby city or state. If you want to test a new vacation idea without investing a lot of time and money, a weekend trip is a perfect solution.

Why not spend a weekend exploring America's past? Preserved and restored reminders of our national history dot the countryside, and can make a child's dull history books take on a new and lasting meaning. While some are blatantly commercial, many historic sites are genuine attempts to recreate the spirit of day-to-day life in colonial and pioneer America. Williamsburg, Virginia is probably the most famous historic restoration, and the one against which all others are judged. A visit of a day or two will give you plenty of time to absorb the gracious 18th-century atmosphere, ride in a horse-

drawn coach, or listen to a harpsichord by candlelight in the elegant great hall of the Royal Governor's Palace. Your children could probably spend twice that time trying out the stocks at the old gaol, watching soldiers load and fire Revolutionary Brown Bess muskets, and visiting the shops where artisans still work with handmade tools. Authentically costumed guides make the town's history come alive. If you can tear yourself away, you might spend some time in nearby Jamestown and Yorktown, places that also played a vital part in the founding of Virginia and the nation.

Like Virginia, New England is a cradle of American history, and a natural choice for your family's historical forays. The old seaport of Mystic, Connecticut is a favorite of would-be sailors of all ages. Here you can spend the day boarding historic sailing ships, browsing through 19th-century lofts and craft shops staffed by artisans, or simply strolling along the picturesque, cobblestoned waterfront. Old Sturbridge Village near Boston has been called the "living museum of New England". The costumed natives, working farm, and rustic buildings will give your children a good idea of what a rural New England village was like

in the years that followed the Revolution.

The notorious history of Salem, Massachusetts is brought to vivid life in that city's new Museum of Witchcraft—guaranteed to chill the blood of every member of the family. Salem is also rich in literary and seafaring history, and older children will relish a visit to Hawthorne's House of Seven Gables, and the Peabody Maritime Museum. Not far off, in Portsmouth, New Hampshire, you can explore Strawberry Banke—a 10-acre reconstruction on the original site of the 17th-century Portsmouth settlement.

Middle and western America also have their share of historic sites. At Greenfield Village near Dearborn, Michigan your family can ride in a horsedrawn carriage or a Model-T Ford, and admire the superb collection of Americana amassed by Henry Ford. In addition to early cars, trains, and planes, there are hundreds of historic buildings brought to Greenfield Village from every corner of the nation. Among them is Thomas Edison's laboratory. At New Harmony in Indiana, you will see the handiwork of America's most successful communal experiment, dating from the 1820's. The Amana Villages in the lush foothills of southeast Iowa are a living museum of early

Left: the Salem Witch
Museum in Massachusetts
brings the stormy period
of the witch hunts alive.

Monticello, home of our third president Thomas Jefferson, is as interesting as it is beautiful. It shows Jefferson's genius for invention and design as well as the political, literary, and scholarly sides of him.

Below : Galena, Ill., has a reenactment of one of the Civil War battles.

German settlers who still follow old ways.

The further west you go, the wilder the history, and the brasher the restorations. Virginia City, Nevada, a mining-turned-ghost town, has been reborn in all its flamboyant splendor. Grandiose gambling saloons, an old-fashioned newspaper—for which Mark Twain once worked—and a crank telephone system recall the town's more prosperous days. Tombstone, Arizona, with its staged "shootouts" in the OK Corral, and its many wooden buildings, will delight your children.

Indian history, too, can be an interesting subject for short family trips. There is a reconstructed Indian village at Tahlequah,

Oklahoma where you can taste Indian food, watch pageants and traditional festivals, and see Indian craftsmen at work. Most Indian reservations have costumed ceremonials, dances, feasts, and celebrations of interest to visitors of all ages. The list could go on and on—San Antonio, the Alamo, Mark Twain Country, presidential homes, southern plantations, historic houses, Revolutionary and Civil War battlefields. Wherever you live, and whatever period of American history interests you, you're likely to find some historic spot within a short drive of your home.

Tired of cars and mechanized travel? Hiking can be the simplest, least expensive, and most rewarding of all family weekend activities. It's a wonderful way to see nature close up, and to pursue special interests like birdwatching, rock or leaf collecting, and the study of wildflowers. All you need for an afternoon or day's hike are comfortable walking shoes, a small knapsack to carry lunch, and extra sweaters. Don't forget some moleskins, an adhesive fabric to put on chafed heels at the first sign of a blister. Even if you're not accustomed to walking any further than the family car, you'll be delighted at how refreshing and invigorating a quiet walk can be. Wherever you live there's bound to be a footpath nearby. New York City alone has more than 1000 miles of well-marked trails within a few hours' drive. Pick a path that's suited to the age of your children and your family's physical stamina, and don't plan to go too far on your first excursion.

If, like many young families, you fall in love with the idea of traveling under your own steam, you might plan an overnight hike. Backpacking—which means you carry everything you need for a night on your back—is fast becoming a national sport. It's popularity is largely due to the development of lightweight equipment, like the modern aluminum or magnesium frame pack, which distributes weight comfortably and evenly over the hips and back. Like everything else, of course, good backpacking equipment is ex-

pensive. Boots, sleeping bag, pack, tent, and cooking gear can run to more than $300. If you'd like to try backpacking without investing such a large sum, rent the major items (about $15 a weekend), and apply the fee to a later purchase if you like.

Two of the finest walking paths in the country are the Appalachian and Pacific Crest trails, which were designated as part of the National Trail System in 1968. The Appalachian Trail is the longest continuous marked trail in the world, stretching from Maine to Georgia. It has more than 200 shelters along its route, most spaced a day's walk apart. In New Hampshire's White Mountains, the Appalachian Mountain Club maintains pleasant huts where you can get lodging, dinner, and breakfast for $11 (about half that for children). In the West, the Pacific Crest Trail extends from Canada to Mexico. Although there are good campsites all along the way, shelters are provided only in well-traveled areas. For information about local trails write to your county or regional conservation departments, or contact a local hiking club. A good general sourcebook is *Hiking and Hiking Trails—A Trails and Trail Activities Bibliography* ($3), available from the Department of the Interior, Washington, D.C.

Remember when bikes were kid stuff? Well, no more. Whether it's our collective ecological conscience, a national passion for healthy exercise, or just the sheer joy of pedaling, today you will find everyone from dowagers and doctors to mayors and movie stars riding bicycles. If your children are old enough to provide their own pedal power, or young enough to ride in a carrier on the back of your bike, then a cycling trip, complete with picnic lunch, is a great idea for a sunny day. Today you can rent any make of

Left: a mock shootout in Tombstone, Ariz. gives a picture of the rough and lawless Old West days. Above: the dignified and symbolic dances of their old culture are sometimes performed on reservations by Indians.

Right: skilled craftsmen in silver, Indians offer their wares at a market.

bicycle by the hour, day, or weekend for a small fee plus deposit. Check the yellow pages under Bicycle Rentals for shops near you, or near the park or pathway you're heading for. It may work out a little cheaper to rent near the spot you will be cycling in.

If you've never ridden anything but a single-speed balloon tire bicycle, try renting a 3-, 5-, or 10-speed bike. You'll be amazed how much easier it is to pedal up hills and cover long distances. It's important to get the right size bike. If a bicycle is too small, it will tire you out quickly; if too large, it can be dangerous. Sit on the bike in your stocking feet, and place your heel on the pedal in the down position. If your leg is straight, then the bike fits. Most children under 12 are too young to operate gearshift and hand brake bicycles, so let them ride their own bikes, or rent one with a coaster brake, the kind you stop by backpedaling. Again it's important that the bicycle you choose be neither too big nor too small for your child.

Bicycle rental shops are also good sources of information on nearby cycling paths, and places your family can ride to safely on a day's trip. Cycling enthusiasts have been lobbying national, state, and local governments for years to give bike riders an even break. The result: today you can ride a 300-mile bikeway in Wisconsin that follows in part an abandoned railroad line far from

into the car, rent or buy a bicycle carrier that attaches to the trunk, and drive out to the countryside. A country outing is fun for a change in any case.

For more adventurous tours, write for a copy of the *North American Bike Atlas* from the American Youth Hostels, 1554 First Avenue, New York, N.Y. 10028 ($2.50 for nonmembers). It lists over 60 interesting one-day and weekend rides around the country, with routes, sights to see, and places to stay. Does a weekend bike trip seem too ambitious for you? Well you'll find that the bulk of the book maps 100 bike tours from a week to a month in duration, in

Left: biking is a healthy and fun-filled activity the whole family can do.

Right: hiking is another thing that all the family can enjoy together—and a weekend is the perfect time for a short jaunt.

the busy highways. In a landmark decision, Oregon recently allocated one per cent of its gasoline taxes for the construction of foot and bike paths, and many cities—including Seattle, Tallahassee, Boston, Boulder, and Palm Springs—maintain bike paths for residents, and provide route maps for bike-riding visitors. If you don't like the idea of cycling in a city, or have no developed bikeways near you, you can pile the family

case you think that a two-day bike trip sounds strenuous.

If your children are too young, or your muscles not ready for a weekend hiking or cycling tour, there are other family outings you can choose from. For animal enthusiasts, a trip to a wildlife refuge, zoo, safari park, or game farm makes for a memorable weekend. The Bureau of Sport Fisheries and Wildlife administers 30,000,000 acres within its

National Wildlife System. These small Edens, dedicated to the restoration and conservation of American wildlife, are found in every state, and almost every animal native to this country—from Texas longhorns to wild buffalo, to Hawaiian albatross, to Arctic seals—can be seen in some part of the system. Of course, the special pleasure of visiting a refuge is that you see the animals in their natural habitat. Many refuges have self-guiding tours you take on foot or by canoe, as well as museums, information centers, and conducted tours by boat and car. For detailed information on refuges near you, write to the Bureau of Sport Fisheries and Wildlife, Department of the Interior, Washington, D.C. 20240, for their leaflet, "The National Wildlife Refuge System." If you're a camera enthusiast, be sure to ask for the pamphlet, "Outstanding Photographic Opportunities

on National Wildlife Refuges." You'll welcome the tips it gives you.

If your family's interests run more to wild or exotic animals, plan a day's outing to your local zoo, or a nearby wild animal park. Over the past few years many zoos have revolutionized their methods of housing and displaying wild animals. The San Diego Zoo, for instance, has a 1800-acre wild animal preserve that allows you to view animals in settings very much like their native habitats. Wild animal parks, another new development

on the wildlife scene, can be found in most areas of the country. New Jersey has its Jungle Habitat, California its Lion Country Safari, Texas its World of Animals, and Florida its Jungle Larry's Safari Land. Most of these parks duplicate the African experience—you stay in your car and watch the animals from a safe vantage point. A favorite trip for families with very young children is a visit to an animal farm or nursery. Here many of the "don't touch" rules are suspended, and children are allowed to

The zoo is a source of endless delight for children—and adults, too, if the truth were known. Most big cities have zoos of their own—some of them constructed on the new open-range plan that eliminates most cages. Other zoos allow children to hold, pet, and cuddle the animals, or offer a thrilling ride on the back of camels or elephants.

pet, cuddle, and feed the animals, which most children love to do.

Looking for old-fashioned amusement? If you've ever caught yourself hankering for an old-time carnival with its thrill-a-minute rides, cotton candy, and side shows, try taking the family to one of the new and imaginative "theme" parks that are popping up around the country. The thrilling rides are still there, but they've been dressed up Disneyland fashion in an aura of fantasy, history, and foreign lands. Best of all, the tawdriness and fear of being taken that often haunt more traditional amusement parks, are missing. However, you pay a stiff admission fee ($4 to $6 for adults, about half that for children) to see movies, explore theme areas, and enjoy the rides and live performers.

Disneyland and Disney World are, of course, the most famous theme parks, and a visit to one of them is the dream of young kids. But if California and Florida are outside your weekend circuit, there are many

other parks to choose from. At Kings Island Park near Cincinnati, your children can explore a street of European architecture, (there's even a replica of the Eiffel Tower), and pose for a picture with Fred Flintstone or Yogi Bear. The Six Flags Parks in St. Louis, Atlanta, and Arlington, Texas have chosen regional history for their themes. In St. Louis, for example, the World's Fair of 1904 has been recreated, complete with turn-of-the-century buildings. The Land of Oz in North Carolina is based on the film version of the famous book, and includes a yellow brick road, tin man, and nine Dorothys singing "Over the Rainbow." At Opryland, USA, in Nashville—which has long been the center for country music—the attraction, of course, is country music, and you can listen to live entertainment all day, including a pig that plays the piano.

What can you do *this* weekend? There's no beginning or end to the list of possibilities. Drive to the country (or the city), browse through antique shops, attend an auction, tour a winery, have a picnic, organize a neighborhood baseball game, fly a kite. Make your own list, and then make one thing on it a reality. Just remember, weekends are precious. They give you a chance to break away from your daily routine, be together with your family, share new experiences, and store up happy memories. Don't let this weekend slip through your fingers like so many others have in the past.

Above: Disneyland is
high on everyone's list
of places to visit for fun
—especially the kids.

Left: the bright lights
and exciting rides of
a carnival or amusement
park appeal to many as
a recreation activity.

Above left: a tour of a
Hollywood movie studio
will show you how differ-
ent the set is from what
you see on the screen.

Right: going to see the
elaborate floats in a
hometown parade makes
for a pleasant day—and
happy childhood memories.

Rainy Day Activities
9

Neither you nor your child probably think of a rainy day as a likely time for fun, or a break in routine. In fact, you may dread it as a time of boredom and nagging questions about "what can I do?" However, there are many new, different, and even exciting things you can do to enjoy the next rainy day.

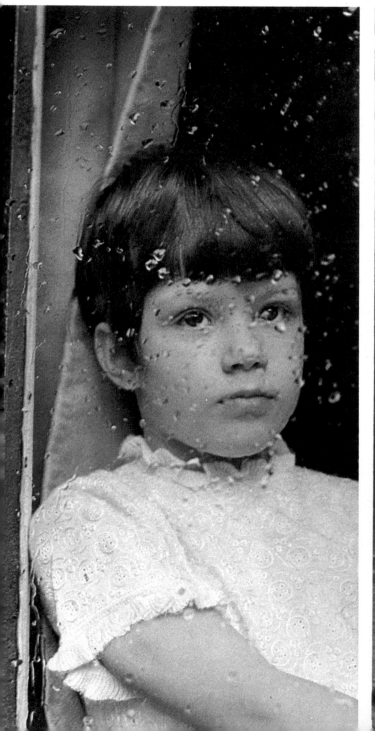

"It's raining, it's pouring . . . ." It's Saturday morning, and all your well-laid plans for a family outing have gone down the drain with the rain. Even before you get out of bed you can anticipate your children's disappointment and restless boredom. Making a rainy day not only bearable, but also fun for the whole family can drive the most ingenious mother to distraction.

This is one instance when urban families have a distinct advantage over their suburban and country cousins. Most big city museums, libraries, theaters, and Y's offer an amazing variety of free or inexpensive indoor activities for children—from puppet making and painting, to films and treasure hunts. But if the weather's simply too bad to venture out, or if there are no preplanned activities in your neighborhood, don't reach for the TV switch in desperation. Try adapt-

ing some of the ideas in this chapter to your family's lifestyle. In addition to helpful hints on filling an hour or two, you might find inspiration for planning your own version of old-fashioned family fun.

One way of curing rainy day blues is to escape into the make-believe world of theater. Most children are hams at heart, and the chance to dress up in costume and put on a show can provide hours of fun for the whole family—audience and actors alike. With a lot of encouragement, and a little

old sheet or bedspread pinned to a clothesline works very well as a curtain, and is usually all it takes to stir a child's imagination. Scenery and props can be as simple as a table and chair, or as elaborate as your children can make them. Why not try painting scenery and larger backdrops on sheets of paper or cardboard (or perhaps you could sacrifice another old sheet)? It's a good way of involving stage-shy youngsters and hesitant fathers in the production.

What child doesn't jump at the chance

Left: putting on make-up for a play can give a child a great deal of pleasure just on its own.

Right: the fun of giving a play doesn't at all depend on expensive or elaborate costumes and props—part of the challenge is doing it with what is around the house.

help from you, even the youngest child will enjoy acting out a beloved nursery rhyme or fairy tale. Older children might prefer writing their own scripts with an original plot, or based on some favorite story or historical incident. There's so much to choose from that one family found their rainy day activity turned into a regular Saturday morning feature that continued, rain and shine, for many years.

"All the world's a stage" may be true for adults, but you'll find that being backstage, and having the curtain go up on a performance is half the fun for most children. An

to dress up as someone else—whether a swashbuckling pirate, a fairy princess, or a young George or Martha Washington. Improvising costumes from old clothes and scraps of material, sporting cotton whiskers and powdered-white hair, and being "made up" are all part of the magic for children.

Variations on home theater activities are endless. Why not hold an impromptu talent show with each person (including mom and dad) performing a skit, song, dance, poem, or magic trick? It's a good chance to let everyone show off what they've learned at school or club, and it doesn't need all the preparation that goes into a full-length drama. If you have a tape recorder, you can tape the show, and delight your children with an instant replay of their own performance. Tapes make fine mementos, too, when the children are grown.

Another favorite family entertainment is the puppet show, which can be easily adapted to your child's age and interests. Teenagers might choose to put on a full-scale marionette show for younger brothers and sisters, or the neighborhood children.

Marionettes can be expensive to buy, take a great deal of time to make, and are fairly difficult to manipulate. Hand puppets, in contrast, are ideal for even the youngest child, and can be made easily from scraps of material, sewn together to make a three-fingered glove, with anything from potatoes to painted papier mache for heads. Making the puppet can often be as much fun as putting on the show itself. A special stage adds immensely to a child's pleasure. A tall, cardboard box—the kind that large

appliances come in—is ideal for a puppet stage, and can be obtained from a local appliance or department store. Just cut out a window on one side, and let your children paint and decorate it themselves. Then, when showtime arrives, they can crouch down or sit on stools inside.

One of the simplest kinds of puppets to make on the spur of the moment is a shadow puppet. All you need is a piece of heavy cardboard and scissors to cut out a figure. Mounted on thin sticks, the puppets can be silhouetted against a screen or sheet illuminated from behind by a high-intensity lamp. If you've ever watched a young child make rabbit's ears on a movie screen, you'll know how fascinating shadow puppets are.

Ask any mother what a child likes to do best on a rainy day, and she'll probably reply, "Make noise." Instead of keeping up a constant refrain of hushes, try turning your children's noisemaking faculties into music making fun. You can make simple musical instruments from many common household items such as pots and pans, tin cans, coat hangers, and boxes of dried beans. The result may still be earsplitting, but in addition to the sheer joy of banging a drum or clanging a cymbal, your children may pick up some fundamentals of rhythm.

Not all indoor activities need be as riotous as an amateur MacNamara's band. If you're looking for a quiet pastime for a late winter afternoon or evening, old-fashioned storytelling can't be bettered. Even jaded teenagers who consider themselves "too old for that sort of thing" have been known to join in with enthusiasm. Make it a special occasion by lighting a fire in the fireplace, letting your youngsters make popcorn, and serving cold or hot drinks. Ghost stories are a favorite with children of all ages, and as long as they're just spooky and not violent or bloody, the chances of their upsetting your children are minimal. (Something that can hardly be said of some television programs.) Even very young tots love the idea of ghosts and goblins as long as there's a warm lap or comforting hand within reach, and older

Below: children love puppet shows, and making the puppets yourselves is not too hard. You don't need any special materials—but imagination will help.

Below right: the puppet theater itself is also very easy to make from wood and cloth scraps, and paint.

children often delight in outdoing one another by dreaming up macabre tales.

Getting your children to make up their own tales is essential to the success of traditional storytelling. A good way to get everyone involved is by starting a round robin story. You or your husband can begin a fable, breaking off at a critical point. The next one in the circle begins where you left off, adding his own twists and turns to the plot. As a pure imaginative exercise, it can't be beat. As your children become more relaxed and accustomed to storytelling, they may want to make up their own stories.

If your spontaneous answer to a child's plaint of "Mommy, what can we do now?" is "Why don't you make something," you'd better be prepared with specific advice and help. Most children are creative once they've

young families is drawing and painting—whether with pen and ink, crayons, finger paints, watercolors, or oils. Since most children love to make pictures, and their art work inevitably ends up on a wall or bulletin board, why not eliminate the middle step and give your child a whole wall to work with? The idea is guaranteed to make a child's eyes light up, and the result can

begun a project, but usually need your guidance and suggestions in order to begin. The variety of arts and crafts you can use to fill a rainy day could fill a book. In fact, it *is* a book in this series. Called *Crafts for Fun and Profit*, it will give you step-by-step instructions on a variety of do-it-yourself projects from *decoupage* to string sculpture, as well as a special section on crafts for children.

A traditional rainy day activity in most

often be a stunning addition to your home. One family, whose children are now grown with youngsters of their own, still treasure a small corner in the basement playroom. The wall, painted during a long, snowbound school holiday when the oldest youngster was 12, is a childhood fantasy of purple lions and pink giraffes inhabiting a weird and wonderful jungle. No one would think of covering it over, and over the years it has become a symbol of fun-filled family days.

Begin by choosing a theme—animals, a carrousel, a favorite nursery rhyme, a landscape—and have each member of the family sketch his ideas on paper. Then you can combine the best of each drawing into one family version. It's usually better if an older person—you, your husband or a teenager—sketches an outline of the plan on the wall. But after that, there should be no preconceived ideas of what a daisy or a dwarf should look like. Everyone can take a turn with paint and brush, using only his

Above : put a few drops of food coloring in glass wax and let your child paint a window. Then the raindrops that beat against it won't matter nearly so much.

Left : ask your child to draw a map of the neighborhood you live in. He won't see it as adults do—and that's what can make it so much fun.

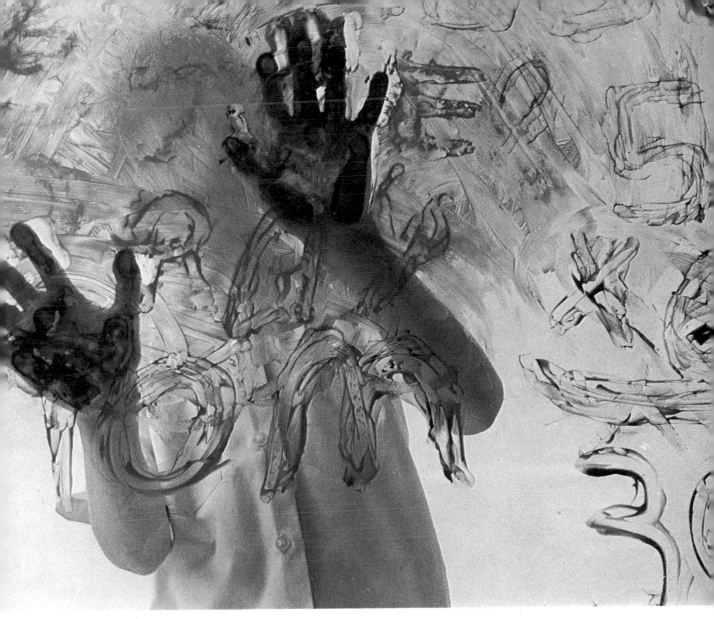

imagination as a guide. If you use a water based paint, you'll find there's less fuss with mixing and cleaning up spills from floors and children.

One theme that can be as startling in its results as in its simplicity is a neighborhood map. Seeing the world through the eyes of a child is often a revelation to grownups. It's a technique frequently used by city planners interested in preserving local landmarks. Don't expect the map to be geographically to scale—the beauty of a child's vision is often in its exaggerations. A long row of houses may be hastily sketched by a few lines, and then suddenly a large red house with a porch and a swing labeled "Tommy's House" will appear. The size of your church or candy store will probably be out of all proportion to the nearby dry cleaners or dress shop, places that have little meaning to a child. In most cases your own home will be at the center of the map, just as it's at the center of your child's world. The whole project can be a source of delight for parents as well as children; and this time the education is usually gained by the adults.

If you'd like to combine rainy day crafts with your next family outing, why not have everybody make a kite? Kite making and kite flying are ancient arts that make marvelous family activities. You can create a kite in a few minutes from folded construc-

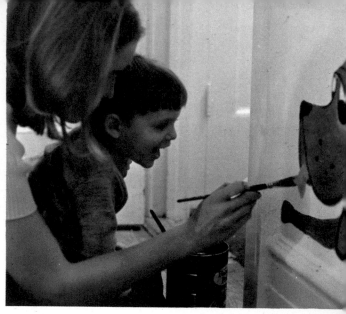

If the thought of turning your child loose with a can of paint and a bare wall makes you nervous, do the project together. You can draw the outlines for him.

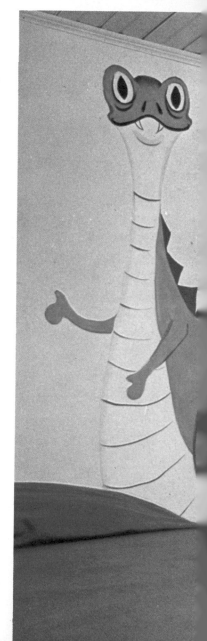

tion paper, with crepe paper for a tail, and thread as string, or you can spend hours or days making your own intricate design. The American Kitefliers Association in Silver City, New Mexico, publishes several kite books and the quarterly *Kite Tales*, which will give you all the basics of building a kite, and making it soar. If you're less ambitious you can buy a standard kite kit in any five-and-ten, and then substitute your own fabric or paper design.

Still another way of putting a rainy day to good use is to get a head start on your next family vacation. Now might be a good time to hold that family "planning session" we mentioned earlier, following up with writing letters to tourist bureaus, reading travel guides, and researching historic sites. Or what about using a rainy afternoon to sort out last year's vacation pictures and post-cards? Making a scrapbook of remembered pleasures can often bring back all the fun of the original trip.

You needn't limit your rainy day travel fun to real trips, past or future. Take a make-believe vacation to a far-off land or exotic place you'll probably never get to visit in reality. The imagination travels infinitely faster than any jet, and is a good deal cheaper. Are you and your family fascinated by the mystery of the Orient? Charter a family adventure to Japan. Get out a map of the Far East, and plan your itinerary. Each child can pick a region or city to explore by checking in the encyclopedia for information on its history, tourist sights, religion, festivals, and customs. Old magazines are often good sources for specialized articles and pictures of famous places. When no photos are available, have your children draw pictures of what they think something might look like from the written description—a pagoda, rickshaw, giant Buddha, or rock landscape. A fun idea is for everyone to make their own postcards from heavy cardboard and magic markers, and then send them off to grandparents and other relatives with a "wish you were here" on the back.

Despite the warnings of sages and weathermen, few of us plan for a rainy day until it arrives; but often it is the spur-of-the-moment activity, born of necessity (and sometimes quiet desperation), that gives your family the most pleasure. Next time it rains or snows, try turning on your family's imagination rather than the television. The results may astound you.

Questions & Answers

Planning a vacation is exciting, especially if you've decided to break out of a rut, and try something new and different this year. But, as we all know, vacation planning doesn't end with that exhilarating moment when you finally decide where and when to go. Like a wedding, the preparations only begin when the proposal is accepted.

Now comes the hectic process of actually getting ready for the great day. There are reservations to make, passports, maps, and guidebooks to be collected, clothing and equipment to be sorted out, tickets and travelers' checks to be picked up, and a thousand-and-one details to be seen to before you can even think of leaving. It's all part of the annual break from routine, and it all helps to build up that special mood of excitement that precedes every vacation. It also adds to the feeling that you—as general planner and organizer of this expedition— are really going to deserve the vacation!

For many people, however it's midway through the flurry of preparations that various doubts and qualms begin to assail them. Supposing someone gets sick? How will the kids react to long hours on the road, or in the air? How do I go through customs? What do I do if I lose my passport? What should we pack? Should we have special vacation insurance? Will buying a car abroad really save money? Should I bargain for purchases in foreign countries? How should I prepare the children for the trip? How can I keep them amused for long hours on the road? What can I do if I lose my airplane ticket? Will I get Montezuma's revenge? These, and other questions should be answered so you can leave for your vacation with an easy mind.

This supplement is designed to answer those questions, and others, that tend to crop up before the vacation begins. It covers health precautions, helpful hints on traveling with children, and ways to stretch the vacation budget. Last, but not least, it includes a listing of state, regional, and international tourist boards to which you may write for free travel information.

Helping you to a carefree vacation for you and your family—free from worries about health, insurance, how much money to take, and even basic questions such as whether you made the right choice of where to go in the first place—is the aim of this book and these questions and answers.

Vacation Spending

Is there any way to determine in advance just how much vacation cash you'll need?

This is the classic vacation quandary. In fact, only those who follow exactly the same vacation pattern year after year can be nearly exact about how much money they'll need. For the rest of us, it's always something of a gamble. It is possible, however, to arrive at a realistic estimation of costs if you really think it out ahead of time.

First, of course, there are the basics: transportation, accommodation, and meals. If you're taking a packaged tour, these will have been paid for in advance. But if you're going to be planning and paying for your holiday as you go along, you'll want to work out your traveling and living expenses very carefully before you set off. Find out as much as you can—from travel agencies, tourist bureaus, and friends who've been to the same area—about hotel and campsite fees, food and drink prices, highway toll fees, the cost of gas, etc.

Next, give some thought to the kind of "extras" your vacation may involve. Will you be wanting to rent a car, take a ferry, visit museums, take special excursions, use private beaches, rent any kind of sporting equipment? Will you be wanting to sample the local nightlife, and do you find it hard to resist souvenirs? Have you got small children with a big appetite for ice cream and soft drinks? Small expenditures have a way of mounting up fast on vacation, and even though they may seem avoidable before you set off, they often become essential to the success of your vacation once you're on your way. This is why, as a general rule of thumb, it's a good idea to add another 10 to 20 per cent to the amount you've already allocated for your vacation, even after you've calculated your basic and "extra" expenses. Unless you are very good at self-denial, you'll probably need every penny of it.

Finally, try to set aside a certain untouchable amount in case of emergency—an unexpected medical expense, for example, or the cost of getting your car repaired. If no such emergency crops up, you'll have the money to take home with you. If it does, you'll thank your lucky stars—and your foresight—for being prepared.

What kind of "hidden costs" are you likely to run into on a packaged tour?

Quite a number of pleasant extras are not included in all-inclusive vacations. For instance, wine with meals, and coffee afterward, are rarely part of the package. Organized excursions will almost certainly be extra during the main summer season, though in winter they are sometimes included in the price of the tour. You will also have to pay for evening entertainment. You may be charged a small sum to attend a dance at your hotel, for example, and you'll certainly be charged admission to the hotel nightclub or discotheque. The admission fee may be reduced for residents, but the price of drinks will not be, and can run high. It's a good idea to check with your tour operator about this kind of extra before you set off.

We enjoy going out—for meals, drinks, nightclub entertainment, etc.—on our vacation, but it's getting more and more expensive. How can we cut costs without giving up such pleasures altogether?

Formal nightlife, with dancing, drinking, and cabaret, tends to be fairly expensive wherever you go these days. So if you like to indulge in a bit of elegant nightclubbing, there isn't really any way to avoid the costs involved. Informal nightlife at discotheques or bars with live music is often less expensive, however, especially if you're willing to look around a bit. It's worth comparing prices. In some places, notably discotheques, the apparently high admission charge also includes your first drink, with subsequent drinks slightly reduced. Again, if you find that drinks at your hotel bar are expensive, and they usually are, search out the smaller bars frequented by the local people. You'll probably pay half the price for the same drinks. Bear in mind that drinks imported into the country—such as wine in Sweden, Scotch whiskey in Italy, or French brandy in Germany—are bound to cost more than those made in the country itself.

Again, when it comes to eating out, be imaginative in your choice of cafes and restaurants. For the privilege of dining in a glittering restaurant on the main thoroughfare, or drinking coffee in some fashionable sidewalk cafe, you may well pay double the price. Seek out places off the beaten track; they'll not only be less expensive, but also a good deal more likely to offer fine cuisine, good service, and authentic local character.

Are you expected to bargain for purchases in foreign countries? If so, what are the rules?

Generally, you don't bargain anywhere in northern Europe, but there are some ex-ceptions. In some markets in France and Belgium, for instance, you can bargain if no prices are indicated on the stall, and the seller seems to be naming a price off the top of his head. You can get a good idea of the real value of the goods for sale by comparing street market prices with those in actual shops; market prices should always be lower than shop prices.

In southern Europe, bargaining is almost always the rule in markets—and sometimes also in shops. The larger, more expensive looking shops always have fixed prices, and some of the others may have a sign in the window reading "prices fixed." But in smaller, cheaper, and more out-of-the-way shops—especially where there are no prices attached to the goods on display, and where the prices quoted seem unreasonably high—it may be all right to bargain. If you're not sure, simply take the plunge, and offer a lower price; the shopkeeper can only say "no."

In North African countries such as Morocco and Tunisia, bargaining is definitely the rule, and is expected of you in all the bazaars. Any North African trader will naturally be pleased to make a massive profit if you pay his initial price, but he will also be disappointed if you haven't engaged him in a bit of artful haggling. So play the game his way.

Look around his shop. Pretend not to be interested in the carpet or copper bowl you want so badly. If you don't know how much you should pay, ask him how much he wants. He will ask double what it's worth. So you have to go the opposite way and offer an absurdly low sum. He will laugh scornfully and pretend to be uninterested. Walk around the shop some more. He will drop his price slightly, and you can raise yours. He may offer you a small cup of mint tea. Take it, but don't feel obliged to buy now, just because he is being kind. It's still all part of the game. If you have the patience, keep the price moving upward ever so slowly, and then stick. Walk down the street if necessary, and go into the shop of a competitor. Then return after several minutes.

You may feel this is a waste of time. If so, and you badly want the item, pay what you think you can afford, and don't have any regrets when you see a similar item somewhere else for half the price. If you're hesitant about bargaining at all, look for a government-run shop that sells high standard arts and crafts. The fixed prices at these shops are higher than those at bazaars, however, and you don't get a chance to practice the ancient art of bargaining for what you want. You may discover you really enjoy it.

What should you watch out for when buying souvenirs?

Most of us like to take home some special item to remind us of our vacation, or to give to a friend or relative. The manufacture and marketing of souvenirs has become a big business over the past years, and many of the items now available are overpriced and badly made. The garish stores that specialize in selling souvenirs are the ones to avoid. If you should go into one of them, look the merchandise over carefully with the same eye for quality you'd use at home. One particular danger to look out for are the dolls, cuddly toys, and straw animals for children. Many of them are merely tacked together with pins that come out quickly, and may cause pain, soon after you have given it to the child.

Is it true that you have to pay to use the beaches in some parts of Europe?

The majority of beaches in Europe are free, but to gain admission to the best ones in certain areas, you do sometimes have to pay. This is true in many parts of southern France, and in the more popular resort areas of Italy. In places like these, you often find that the public beaches, although free, are not particularly desirable. They are often badly kept, or very small and crowded. Your alternative, if you want more space and comfort, is to head for one of the private beaches in the same area. The set sum charged at this type of beach covers entry, changing facilities (there's usually an attendant, whom you should tip), and such amenities as the use of an umbrella and a chair.

Will we save money by buying a car abroad and shipping it home?

What with payments for ocean transportation, marine insurance, U.S. taxes, foreign license plates, and insurance, you will probably break even, or only realize a small saving by purchasing a car abroad. The one big advantage, of course, is that you need not rent a car while in Europe. Unless you are planning on buying a European car anyway, however, or will be driving on the continent for several months, the headaches and red tape involved in shipping a car home might not be worth it.

If you do decide to purchase, the AAA will give you excellent advice on factory prices, foreign requirements, federal and state import taxes, and shipping problems. It's probably best to arrange your purchase through your local foreign car dealer, who can take care of the paperwork, arrange a trade-in on your old car, and help with foreign registration and license plates. This will also ensure better service once you get the car home.

What happens if you have to cancel your vacation?

If you have a packaged tour or chartered flight, and you find that you have to change your plans, try to cancel as far ahead as possible. Last-minute cancellations on packaged tours can mean a forfeiture of up to 90 per cent of the total cost. If you must return before the date of your chartered flight, you will lose your full one-way fare. When booking your trip or flight, find out about tour and charter flight insurance. Depending on how much coverage you buy, you will be reimbursed for any nonrefundable fees if you have to cancel because of *personal* sickness or injury. Continental Casualty Company of Chicago, Illinois can give you information on this type of insurance.

Health Problems

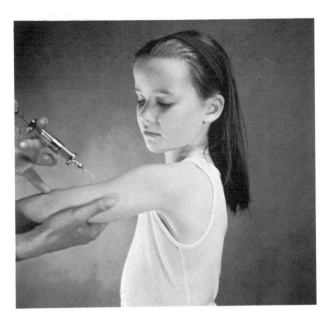

What immunizations should the family have before going on vacation?

This depends on your itinerary. While the USA no longer requires a smallpox vaccination if you go to Western Europe, trips outside this area often require special immunizations. Send for the U.S. Public Health Service publication No. 384, "Immunization for International Travel," for complete information on USA and foreign requirements.

As a basic precaution—for health at home as well as abroad—it is always wise to make sure that your children have been immunized against smallpox, tetanus, diphtheria, and polio. If it has been many years since you or your older children received these immunizations, consult your doctor. He may well advise booster shots. Remember that travelers, often overtaxing themselves with hectic activities, and eating unfamiliar foods in an unfamiliar climate, are more vulnerable to infection than stay-at-homes.

If possible, try to have all necessary immunizations completed a month or two before departure. The later you leave it, the more chance there is that some recently innoculated member of the family will still be feeling the after-affects when the trip gets underway.

What other medical precautions should you take before your vacation?

Second only to making sure that everyone—and especially the children—is properly immunized against serious diseases, you should reassure yourself on the score of your family's present health. Any lingering coughs or colds, skin irritations or unhealed cuts and grazes, persistent indigestion or bowel trouble, should be talked over with the doctor before you leave. It's no good saying to yourself that a few days in the sun will work wonders. Minor ailments can turn into major problems when you are away from home, and wanting to feel your best. It's a good idea, too, to make sure that everyone has had a dental checkup well in advance of departure. A toothache can make a misery of even the sunniest day.

If you or any member of the family is under treatment for a chronic sickness, be sure to get your physician to write a prescription for enough medicine to last you through the trip. If you wear glasses, take a spare pair along with you if possible. This is even more imperative if you are going to be doing some or all of the driving, or if you have small children whose activities you have to watch over.

Is it safe for a woman to travel by air when she is pregnant?

The safety of air travel for a pregnant woman depends on two factors: first, the month of her pregnancy, and second, her general state of health. Air travel is unadvisable after seven months of pregnancy. In fact, because of the risk of a premature birth at this stage, most airlines insist that the woman obtain

133

a doctor's certificate before making the journey. If a woman is in the last two weeks of her pregnancy, an airline is entitled to refuse her permission to fly at all. This rarely happens, of course, because few women are likely to attempt a trip at this point except in an emergency.

An expectant mother's general health and medical history enter the picture, too. At any stage in her pregnancy, she would be wise to consult her doctor before undertaking a plane journey, just to be certain that it involves no risk for her.

Is it safe to drink local water in foreign countries?

Generally speaking, the drinking water in most tourist resorts is safe to drink. If the other facilities are of a high standard, the water is likely to be as well. If you have any doubts about it, however, you can drink and brush your teeth in mineral water. In this case, make sure that the seal on the bottle is intact when you buy it. Alternatively, you can take a supply of water sterilization tablets with you. These can be obtained from a druggist, and usually have to be put in the water several minutes before it is drunk. If you are camping, or have a small immersion heater with you, you can, of course, boil the water first. You'll have to do so anyway if you are traveling with a baby. Finally, if all else fails, you can confine your intake of liquid to beer, wine, and bottled soft drinks.

What kinds of foods might be suspect in a foreign country?

Wherever you go, it's best to stick to thoroughly cooked and freshly prepared meats, fish, poultry, and vegetables. Eat no raw fruit unless it has an unbroken skin, and you can peel it before eating it. Ice cream can sometimes be a problem. It's wise to be on the safe side, and buy it from street or beach vendors only when it is wrapped. Ice cream can also be eaten safely if bought from cafes with good refrigeration facilities. Refrigeration is also an important consideration when buying cream or custard-filled pastries; meat, fish, or potato salads; cold egg mixtures; or sliced cold meats. It's wise to avoid these particularly perishable items in hot countries unless you can be absolutely sure that they have come straight from the refrigerator.

Finally, choose your restaurants carefully. As at home, the cleaner and better kept they are, the safer their food will be. It's really a matter of common sense; there's no reason to lower your standards, or to be over-finicky, just because you're in a strange place.

Is there any way to avoid coming down with Montezuma's Revenge?

There are various antidiarrhetic medicines on the market now designed to "stop it before it begins," or bring it to a quick halt if it has already started. No one has yet proved whether this abdominal upset is caused by an infection of the intestinal track, or simply by a change in food and climate. There is no doubt, though, that this ailment—usually lasting about three days, and often accompanied by abdominal cramps, nausea, and vomiting—is the single most common complaint of travelers the world over.

To give you some idea of just how widespread it is, here are a few of the humorous names it is known by: Gippy Tummy, Delhi Belly, Hong Kong Dog, Tokyo Trots, and Aztec Twostep. Of course, it's far from funny when you have it, so be sure to equip yourself with a preventive or remedy before you set off. For those traveling in southern Europe, where diarrhea is more likely to strike, it might be a good idea to begin taking the medicine as directed on the package, when you begin your vacation, or just before, if so advised.

What's the best way to avoid getting too much sun too early in the vacation?

Naturally it's wise to protect your own and your children's skin with sun screening creams and/or lotions. But even these will not provide sufficient protection under certain conditions, and certainly not at the beginning of your vacation. Far too many pallid vacationers, with only two short weeks in the sun ahead of them, try to acquire a healthy tan too fast, and wind up with a painful burn. One of the reasons why people go on making this mistake is that the symptoms of a real sunburn often only show up hours after the damage has been done. In severe cases, the painful reddening and blistering may be accompanied by headache, dizziness, exhaustion, and nausea. If this has occurred, the best remedy is to cover the burned areas with calomine lotion, drink more liquids, and rest in the shade. Stay out of the sun till the burn is better.

It's far better to avoid the painful symptoms of sunburn altogether. At the start of the vacation, 15 minutes is plenty of time for the first sunbathing session. After that, it can be increased day-by-day until, by the end of those two precious weeks, you are soaking up the sun safely the whole day long. It's also wise to bear in mind—particularly at the start of the holiday—that the power of the sun's rays is very much intensified when reflected off sand, sea, and snow.

What items should be in a first aid kit for a family vacation?
Your basic check list should include: motion sickness preventives; antidiarrhea tablets; milk of magnesia for minor stomach upsets; a mild laxative; aspirin; throat lozenges; a thermometer; water sterilization tablets; sun screening creams or lotions; calomine lotion; insect repellent and insecticidal spray; a wasp and bee sting preparation; antihistamine cream; waterproof bandages of various sizes and a packet of sterile gauze for cuts and grazes; antiseptic cream; three-inch Ace bandage for sprains; and safety pins, small scissors, and a roll of cotton.

How do you find a doctor abroad?
The U.S. embassy or consulate in the city you are visiting will provide you with lists of approved, English-speaking doctors. There is also a new organization called Intermedic, which assures its members of immediate help by qualified physicians all over the world. The annual membership fee is $5 for an individual, and $9 for a family. Intermedic guarantees maximum fees of $8 for the first office visit, $10 for a daytime hotel house call, and $15 for a nighttime house call. It is located at 777 Third Avenue, New York, N.Y. 10017. The International Association for Medical Assistance to Travelers offers a similar service. The address is 745 Fifth Avenue, New York, N.Y. 10022.

If you become ill in Great Britain or other countries with a socialized health program, you are often cared for at little or no expense, even though you are a foreigner.

What is the best precaution against insect bites, and how dangerous is the sting of a jellyfish?
On a summer vacation, mosquitoes are the most troublesome insect you will usually encounter. Short of remaining constantly surrounded by a cloud of cigarette smoke or aerosol insect repellent, neither of which is very good for you, your best protection against the itchy bites of mosquitoes is to coat your skin with a mild insect repellent. A baby in a cot or carriage can be protected with a covering of mosquito netting. If you are bitten in spite of precautions, apply calomine lotion, eau-de-cologne, or a sparing amount of an antihistamine cream. Wasp and bee stings can be treated with one of the special preparations now on the market. They usually ease the pain quickly.

The sting of most types of jellyfish is somewhat painful, but not dangerous. However, stings of types found in warm seas, such as the Mediterranean, can be. One of the more notorious varieties is the Portuguese Man-O'-War, which is bluish in color, and tends to swim about in shoals. If you see any in the water, get out quickly. Their sting is not only extremely painful, but powerful enough to send the victim into shock. If you are bitten, apply calomine lotion or an antihistamine cream, and, if a fever develops, call a doctor.

Insurance

What kind of auto insurance will we need when driving outside the USA?

Third party insurance is compulsory when driving in Europe, in the form of a standard International Insurance Certificate, or "green card." If you are renting a car, this coverage will be included automatically in the rental fee. Full, nondeductible coverage is usually optional, but is well worth the extra cost. If you are buying or leasing a car in Europe, check with the AAA on purchasing a green card, as well as further coverage. You can't be too careful about getting adequate auto insurance.

Even as close to home as Canada and Mexico, your U.S. insurance might be inadequate or invalid. When driving in Canada, carry the special yellow card available from your insurance agent. This is proof that you have enough liability insurance to meet provincial demands. In Mexico, don't drive at all without proof of liability insurance issued by a licensed Mexican agency. Standard U.S. policies do not apply in Mexico, and if you have an accident, your car may be impounded, and you may be jailed. You can buy special, short-term Mexican insurance at the border, through the AAA, or from your own agent before you start the trip.

We have a general family insurance policy. Is it really necessary to get special vacation insurance as well?

Yes. Vacation insurance policies are geared to the kind of away-from-home difficulties that general policies simply do not cover. Too many people overlook this important safeguard before going on vacation, and find

out only too late that they might have been saved a monstrous bill if they'd been prepared. Special trip insurance is, of course, like taking an umbrella. If you have it, you probably won't need it; but if you don't, it's more likely to be needed.

It's a simple matter these days to obtain comprehensive special trip insurance for every member of the family. Most of the larger insurance firms offer short-term vacation policies whose premiums vary with the length of the vacation. For example, a three-week accidental injury policy costing about $34 per person covers the following: $50,000 in life insurance benefits; $5,000 in medical and surgical benefits; $200 a day for hospitalization of up to two months, and reimbursement for dismemberment. Family members under 16 qualify for reduced benefits. You can insure your family's personal effects and baggage for up to $2,000 at a cost of about $21 for the same period. That's not much to pay for peace of mind.

Be sure to read the policy carefully. If expensive medical treatment should be needed away from home, and the problem is a pre-existing one, the insurance firm is not liable. The same is true, of course, of any policy taken out after the start of some serious medical problem. Consult your agent for advice on this important matter.

Children on Vacation

What's the best way to prepare small children for their first trip?

As many parents have discovered, the most successful approach is not to prepare them at all. In other words, make as little fuss about going away as you possibly can. To a small child, the word "vacation" has no meaning—unless and until his parents give it one with endless, incomprehensible details, last-minute panics, and a general build-up of hectic anticipation. The very idea of leaving home and going to a strange place can create anxiety in a child, particularly if his parents are in a high state of excitement about it. The answer, therefore, is to keep the pre-vacation tempo at a low key. When telling small children about the coming trip, and it's not necessary to do so weeks in advance, mention it calmly, as though it were an everyday matter. If they tend to be nervous or excitable, try to do the packing out of sight. As with most things, a child will take his emotional cues from his parents, so the less upset they seem, the less upset he will be.

How can you prevent travel sickness in young children?

There are several ways to reduce the likelihood of their suffering from it. First, try to avoid a build-up of last-minute tension; excitement is at the root of most travel sickness. Second, make sure that the meals eaten before and during the journey are light, sustaining, and fat-free. A heavy meal of fried foods is just asking for trouble. Third, if your experience tells you that the children are prone to motion sickness, consult your doctor about a suitably mild preventive medicine,

and give it to them before you set off. There's no use waiting until they begin to turn green —by that time, it's too late for the remedy to take affect. One pleasant side effect of these mild children's travel sickness remedies is drowsiness. This can be a great help, especially if you're traveling at night, and want to get the kids to sleep so that they'll arrive refreshed after the journey. Finally, try to restrain yourself from asking them how they feel. Travel sickness in small children can all too easily be psychologically induced by overanxious parents. When asked questions like, "Are you all right, dear?" "Are you sure you're feeling well?" a child may discover a distressing symptom.

What can you do to keep children amused during the journey?

Whether traveling by car, plane, ship, or rail, a long journey in an enclosed space can be exceedingly wearing, for both children and parents. The novelty of the situation soon wears off, and the problem of keeping the little ones busy and happy can loom large. But there are many things you can do to help your youngsters while away the time. One tried-and-true gimmick it to take along a series of "mystery bags". Depending on the ages of the children, these can be filled with all kinds of surprises—small books both old and new, a scribbling pad or magic slate, a hand puppet, a favorite toy truck or cuddly stuffed animal, coloring books, puzzles, inexpensive little knickknacks from the toy shop. The mystery bags can be brought out at strategic intervals throughout the trip, and simply guessing what might be in the next one can take up some time. After they've been opened and the contents played with and discarded, the various items in the bags can be wrapped up again to be used again later. The same is true of all the playthings, personal comforters, and so forth, brought along on the journey. A small child gets bored very quickly, and the toys he is tired of playing with at one moment may be welcomed with fresh delight an hour or so later.

On any journey, games and storytelling can do a lot to make the time go by more quickly for both children and parents alike. Travel games, of course, depend a lot on the ages of your children, and on what mode of transportation you're using. Some of the games you can play in a car for example, are not possible in a plane—you can't count horses from 30,000 feet. But even in a plane, it's surprising how many variations you can make on old favorites like "I spy." With very young children, this game can be played with colors instead of words. ("I spy, with my little eye, something colored red.") Another game is to take turns at guessing a word. Someone says, "I'm thinking of a word that rhymes with feet." The others will try "heat," or "seat," or "street," and whoever gets the one the first person had in mind— say "street"—takes the next turn.

If you're traveling by car, there are all kinds of observation games you can play by dividing the travelers up into those on the right- and left-hand sides of the car. How many horses, cows, sheep, dogs, ladies with hats, houses with red roofs, etc., can you see on your side of the road within a given period of time?

It's difficult for children to restrain their high spirits, and they need to move about a bit while traveling. You can help them relieve the tension of sitting still by singing songs accompanied by hand clapping, or by playing games such as "Simon says." ("Hands on head," "Hands on knees," "Hands behind your back," "Hands over your ears," etc.) It can be fun to restrict this versatile game to the face alone. ("Eyes up," "Eyes down," "Eyes left," "Eyes right," "Happy face," "Sad face," "Mad face," "Silly face," etc.) The results will probably have you all in giggles. If you don't already know these sing-song or nonsense games, your children are likely to have learned them at school. It makes for entertainment if they teach you how the game songs go.

What about feeding infants en route?
If the baby is still being breastfed, the only problem is securing privacy when it's time to feed him. Most airports have nurseries with rooms for nursing mothers, and it's usually possible to find some private corner in airplanes, trains, and stations.

If the baby is bottle-fed, you can use one of several different methods to give him a warm meal. First, you can prepare all the bottles he'll need during the journey, plus an extra in case of a delay, cool them down with the nipples reversed, and pack them away for reheating en route. Reheating can be done with a large thermos of hot water and a jug. It's a good idea to take your own hot water, because it's not always possible to acquire it when and where you need it. On planes, for example, stewardesses will normally be happy to supply a jug of hot water for bottle heating. But on busy holiday flights, they may be so occupied serving meals and drinks to demanding adults that you might have to wait too long.

With a thermos of hot water—boiled first to sterilize it—you can also employ a second, easier method of making a warm meal. Simply take the necessary number of empty, sterilized bottles, with the nipples reversed, and a supply of dried milk. Then, when it's feeding time, you need only mix the dried milk with the hot water. Still another method, again requiring empty, sterilized bottles and a thermos of sterilized hot water, is to take along a supply of evaporated milk, and mix up the formula when required. Use any of the above methods in preference to heating the baby's milk in advance, and hoping that it will stay warm and sterile en route.

If you have a small toddler, you'll want to take milk or fruit juice (and his favorite cup), together with a thermos of hot water, and a supply of strained or instant baby foods to heat or mix as needed. Airlines often have baby foods on hand, but it's just as well not to count on it.

Contrary to many people's fears, parents in other countries feed their babies and toddlers the same kinds of foods we do. Ideal, Carnation, and Nestle's evaporated milk are available in almost every country in Western Europe. The same is true of Heinz and Gerber baby foods. Occasionally, these old standbys are sold under different brand names—for example, Carnation is known as Gloria in France, and as Gluksi in Germany; Heinz is known as Plasman in Italy. There are also dozens of perfectly safe local brands. The only point to be particularly careful about is the butterfat content in foreign-made evaporated milk. It can be higher than your usual brand, so you should read the instructions about diluting it carefully.

What about the baby's other needs while traveling by air?

If you're traveling by air, and don't have your own portable cot, you may want to reserve one ahead of time for use during the journey. Even if you have a cot, you may well want to reserve a rack to hold it, rather than putting it on the floor, or on your lap. The "sky cots" and racks are designed for babies up to 12 months old.

Disposable diapers are not always available on the plane, so be prepared with a supply. You'll also need a plastic bag of premoistened absorbent cotton, and another plastic bag for used diapers, discarded tissues, etc. Don't pack away the baby's pacifier if he's used to having it.

General

Are there any general rules on packing for a family vacation?

This is probably the most often-asked travel question. The answer, of course, largely depends on the type and length of vacation you will be taking. But, as a rule, the key to easier packing is to take as little as possible.

All airlines have strict baggage allowances (44 lbs. on an economy ticket), and charge high for each pound over the limit. Although there is almost no restriction on what you can take aboard a cruise ship, you will still find excess luggage a handicap in terms of cramped cabin space, and endless packing and unpacking.

A good rule of thumb is to take only what you can carry yourself, which will not only save on porters' tips, but will also help speed you through customs. Then, too, you will want to have room for purchases you make during the trip.

Find out what the weather will be like where you are going, and, accordingly, try to limit each member of your family to a few changes of clothing. Make sure everything you pack, especially children's clothes, can be cared for easily. Dry cleaning and pressing are expensive and time-consuming all over the world.

Don't take anything of great value, such as expensive jewelry or furs. You will probably spend half your vacation guarding it, and the other half worrying about it. If you are going abroad, don't pack electrical appliances such as a razor, travel iron, or hairdryer, unless they operate on the higher foreign voltage.

If you are traveling by air, do not pack aerosol cans or book matches in your luggage, because they create danger of explosion or combustion at high altitudes.

Do not pack exposed or unexposed film in your luggage, either. It is likely to be ruined by the X-rays now used in security procedures at international airports.

How do we arrange to get mail while abroad?

If your reservations and itinerary are confirmed, you can have mail sent directly to the hotels at which you will be staying. The letters should be clearly marked, "Hold for arrival on such and such a date." Remember, Europeans write the date with the day first, and then the month and year. Thus 7/6/74 is the 7th of June 1974. When in doubt, tell your family and friends to write the date out. If you have no advance reservations, you can use the mail services of American Express or Thomas Cook travel agencies. You will be required to show travelers checks as well as your passport for identification. Be prepared to wait on long lines at American Express offices during the summer season.

How do you choose a guidebook?

Choosing a guidebook is almost as personal as picking a traveling companion, and often as important. Even if you are traveling as part of a guided tour, you will still find a good written guide an important part of your trip abroad. Whatever your idea of fun—history, culture, shopping sprees, nightlife, or little-known backroads—there's sure to be a guidebook keyed to your specific interests. J. A. Neal's *Reference Guide for Travelers* gives a description of virtually every guidebook available in the USA, and is worth consulting before making your selection. Whichever you choose, buy it well in advance of the trip, and bone up on what you will be seeing before you leave.

Probably the best and most popular general guides are the *Michelin Red Guide* or *Green Guide* to individual countries. The *Green Guide* is famous for its rating of outstanding sights. It also gives excellent historical and cultural backgrounds to each country, as well as detailed practical information on locations, open hours, fees, etc. The *Red Guide* to restaurants and hotels is equally outstanding, and will lead you to the finest of European cuisines. Both guides are slim paperbacks, the size of a legal envelope, and can be easily toted.

One of the best sources of information on European hotels, restaurants, and shopping for budget-minded families is Fielding's *Super Economy Guide to Europe*. It is crammed full of money-saving tips, and the establishments listed are updated each year. The introduction, too, offers excellent, down-to-earth information on transportation, tipping, customs, camping, and such topics.

What should we know about clearing U.S. customs?

When you return to the United States, you are required to make a written or oral declaration of all articles acquired abroad—even if received as a gift, or used while traveling. You will receive a card for this purpose before you land.

If your purchases total $100 or less, you pay no import duty at all, provided you have been outside the country for at least 48 hours, the articles are for your personal or household use, and that they accompany you. Items shipped or mailed home are subject to duty and tax. You can, however, send an unlimited number of duty-free *gifts*, costing less than $10 each, to friends without effecting your personal $100 exemption. The only requirement is that no more than one package a day is sent to the same person. All purchases over the $100 exemption are taxable at from 1 to 50 per cent of the retail value.

Families traveling together may combine their exemptions, which means that a child or infant's exemption can be applied to your own purchases. You must be over 21 (18 in New York) to bring in alcoholic beverages, and you are restricted to one quart per individual. There is no limit to the amount of cigarettes you can bring in, but only 100 cigars (of non-Cuban origin) are allowed.

Among articles or products you cannot bring into the country are food, plants, or animals without special permission from the Department of Agriculture; articles made in Cuba, North Korea, North Vietnam or Southern Rhodesia; certain items considered injurious or detrimental to the general welfare of the USA (i.e. narcotics, obscene literature, lottery tickets, liquor-filled candies); and certain trademarked articles. For detailed information on customs regulations, send for "Customs Hints for Returning U.S. Residents" (10 cents) from the Superintendent of Documents, Government Printing Office, Washington, D.C. 20402.

If your camera, watch, or other such article is foreign made, register it with customs officials before leaving the country, or you may have to pay duty on it when you return.

What about customs and duty abroad?

Clearing foreign customs is usually much easier than U.S. clearance. Most officials are chiefly concerned that the amount of cigarettes, alcohol, and perfume you are bringing into the country is for personal consumption only. The amounts vary from place to place, but most allow visitors 200 to 400 cigarettes, one or two quarts of alcohol, and one bottle of perfume. Anything in excess of the duty-free limit must be declared, and is liable to duty or confiscation, so check on limits before you enter a particular country.

Many airports have introduced a new system to speed up customs clearance. If you have nothing to declare, you pass through a specially designated exit. Although you are still liable to a spot check, your chances for getting through quickly are much greater.

What should you do if you lose your air ticket or passport?

In the case of a lost ticket, report it immediately to your airline. Your name will be on their passenger list, and they will issue you

a new ticket. In the case of a lost passport, report it immediately to the local police, and to the nearest American consular office, which will issue you a temporary passport. Be warned that the process may take several days.

What should we know about renting a car and driving in Europe?

If a car is not a part of a package deal, you will probably save money by waiting until you arrive in Europe to make your rental arrangements. Local agencies often offer special discounts and lower rates than are available through international firms. If you prefer the convenience of having a car waiting at the airport, you can arrange a rental before leaving home through the AAA, Hertz, or Avis.

The cheapest cars advertised are always standard shift, economy models. If you insist on an automatic American car, you will pay considerably more. Small European cars are better suited for driving on narrow, country lanes and medieval city streets, and have the added advantage of using less gas. Also, gasoline costs in Europe are as much as three times what they are at home. Some countries, such as Italy, issue special tourist gas coupons offering reductions of up to 30 per cent. In most cases they must be purchased before you enter the country. Check with the AAA for detailed information.

Your current U.S. driver's license is valid in most Western European countries. Some countries, among them Spain, Portugal, Austria, Greece, and Turkey, require an International Driving Permit. Even when not required, the permit is a smart investment because it is in several languages, and can be interpreted easily by border officials and local police. It can be obtained from the AAA for a fee of $3.

While European roads are generally good, they don't compare with U.S. highways, so don't expect to cover as much mileage as you would in the same amount of time at home. In Great Britain and Ireland, you drive on the left-hand side of the road.

Teenage Holiday Addresses

Bureau of Publicity and
Information
State Highway Building
Montgomery, Ala. 36104

Alaska Travel Division
Pouch E
Juneau, Alaska 99801

Department of Economic
Planning and Development
3003 N. Central Ave.
Phoenix, Ariz. 85012 and
Department of Travel and
Information
Phoenix, Ariz. 85005

Department of Parks and
Tourism
101 State Capitol
Little Rock, Ark. 72201

Office of Tourism and Visitors
Service
1400 Tenth St.
Sacramento, Calif. 95814

Additional tourist information
sources for California:
Northern California:

San Francisco Convention and
Visitors Bureau
Fox Plaza
San Francisco, Calif. 94102

Redwood Empire Association
476 Post St.
San Francisco, Calif. 94102

Shasta-Cascade Wonderland
Association
Box 155
Redding, Calif. 96002

Southern California:

Southern California Visitors
Council
705 W. 7th St.
Los Angeles, Calif. 90017

San Diego Convention and
Visitors Bureau
225 Broadway
San Diego, Calif. 92101

California Mission Country
Visitors Association
25 W. Anapamu St.
Santa Barbara, Calif. 93104

Colorado Visitors Bureau
225 Colfax Ave.
Denver, Colo. 80202

Colorado State Division
of Commerce and
Development
602 State Capitol Annex
Denver, Colo. 80203

Denver Visitors Bureau
Denver, Colo. 80202

Connecticut Development
Commission
Box 865
Hartford, Conn. 06115

Travel Development Bureau
45 The Green
Dover, Del. 19901

Bureau of Marketing and
Tourism
107 West Gaines St.
Tallahassee, Fla. 32304

Miami Metro Department
of Publicity and
Tourism
499 Biscayne Blvd.
Miami, Fla.

Georgia Department of
Industry and Trade
Box 38097
Atlanta, Ga. 30334

Hawaii Visitors Bureau
2270 Kalakaua Ave.
Honolulu, Hawaii 96815

Idaho Department of Commerce
and Development
State Capitol Building
Room 108
Boise, Idaho 83707

Illinois Department
of Business and
Economic Development
222 South College Ave.
Springfield, Ill. 62706

Chicago Convention and
Tourism Bureau
332 South Michigan Ave.
Chicago, Ill. 60604

Indiana Department of
Commerce
323 State House
Indianapolis, Ind. 46204

Iowa Development Commission
250 Jewett Building
Des Moines, Iowa 50309

Department of Economic
Development
Room 1225
Topeka, Kan. 66612

Kentucky Department of Public
Information
Capitol Annex
Frankfort, Ky. 40601

Tourist Development
Commission
Box 44291
Baton Rouge, La. 70804

Greater New Orleans
Tourist and Convention
Commission
334 Royal St.
New Orleans, La. 70130

Department of Economic
Development
State House
Augusta, Maine 04330

Division of Tourism
State Office Building
Annapolis, Md. 21401

Department of Commerce and
Development
100 Cambridge St.
Boston, Mass. 02202

Boston Convention and
Visitors Bureau
125 High St.
Boston, Mass. 02202

Michigan Tourist Council
Stevens I. Mason Building
Lansing, Mich. 48926

Minnesota Department of
Economic Development
51 East 8th St.
St. Paul, Minn. 55101

Agricultural and Industrial
Board
Box 849
Jackson, Miss. 39205

Missouri Tourism Commission
Box 1055
Jefferson City, Mo. 65101

Montana Highway
Commission
Helena, Mont. 59601

Nebraska Department of
Economic Development
State Capitol
Lincoln, Neb. 68509

Department of Economic
Development
State Capitol
Carson City, Nev. 89701

Division of Economic
Development
Box 856
Concord, N.H. 03301

Division of Economic
Development
Box 5400
Trenton, N.J. 08625

Department of Development
113 Washington Ave.
Santa Fe, N. Mex. 87501

State Department of Commerce
112 State St.
Albany, N.Y. 12207

New York Convention and
Visitors Bureau
90 E. 42nd St.
New York, N.Y. 10017

For recorded phone message on
citywide activities call:
Parks, Recreation, and
Cultural Affairs Administration:
Manhattan, Bronx: 755-4100
Brooklyn, Queens, Staten
Island: 691-5858
Park Events: 472-1003

For a book on attractions in
New York City, write:
"PRCA Where Book"
830 Fifth Ave.
New York, N.Y. 10021 (10c)

Department of Conservation
and Development
Box 27687
Raleigh, N.C. 27611

North Dakota Highway
Department Building
Travel Division
Bismark, N.Dak. 58501

Ohio Department of
Development
Box 1001
Columbus, Ohio 43216

Oklahoma Tourist and
Information Division
500 Will Rogers Memorial
Building
Oklahoma City, Okla. 73105

Oregon State Highway Division
101 State Highway Building
Salem, Ore. 97310

Oregon Coast Association
Drawer 1266
Newport, Ore. 97365

Bureau of Travel Development
Pennsylvania Department of
Commerce
Harrisburg, Pa. 17120

Philadelphia Convention and
Tourist Bureau
1525 John F. Kennedy Blvd.
Philadelphia, Pa. 19102

Rhode Island Development
Council
207 Roger Williams Building
Providence, R.I. 02908

Department of Parks,
Recreation and Tourism
Box 1358
Columbia, S.C. 29202

Department of Highways
Travel Section Communications
Pierre, S. Dak. 57501

Black Hills, Badlands, and
Lakes Association
Sturgis, S. Dak. 57785

Department of Conservation
2611 W. End Ave.
Nashville, Tenn. 37203

Texas Tourist Development
Agency
Box 12008, Capitol Station
Austin, Tex. 78711

Travel Council
Council Hall, State Capitol
Salt Lake City, Utah 84114

Travel Development
61 Elm St.
Montpelier, Vt. 05602

Virginia State Travel Service
911 East Broad St.
Richmond, Va. 05602

Washington Department of
Commerce and Economic
Development
General Administration
Building
Olympia, Wash. 98501

Seattle Visitors Bureau
215 Columbia St.
Seattle, Wash. 98104

Washington D.C. Convention
and Visitors Bureau
1129 – 20th St. N.W.
Washington D.C. 20036

West Virginia Department of
Commerce
1900 Washington St. E.
Charleston, W. Va. 25305

Department of Natural
Resources
Box 450
Madison, Wisc. 53701

Wyoming Travel Commission
2320 Capitol Ave.
Cheyenne, Wyo. 82001

Tourist Board Addresses

British Tourist
Authority
680 Fifth Ave.
New York, N.Y. 10019

Quebec Government House
Travel Information Bureau
17 W. 50th St.
New York, N.Y. 10020

French Government Tourist
Office
610 Fifth Ave.
New York, N.Y. 20020

Irish Tourist Board
590 Fifth Ave.
New York, N.Y. 10036

Luxembourg Economic and
Tourist Department
200 E. 42nd St.
New York, N.Y. 10017

Mexican National Tourist
Council
677 Fifth Ave.
New York, N.Y. 10022

Netherlands National Tourist
Office
576 Fifth Ave.
New York, N.Y. 10036

Spanish National Tourist Office
589 Fifth Ave.
New York, N.Y. 10017

Swedish National Travel Office
505 Fifth Ave.
New York, N.Y. 10017

Swiss National Tourist Office
608 Fifth Ave.
New York, N.Y. 10020

Venezuelan Government
Tourist Bureau
485 Madison Ave.
New York, N.Y. 10022

Picture Credits